Disclaimer: This book serves to be a general guide for our recovery program. The actual program schedule and content can and will be adjusted to meet your needs.

I0559589

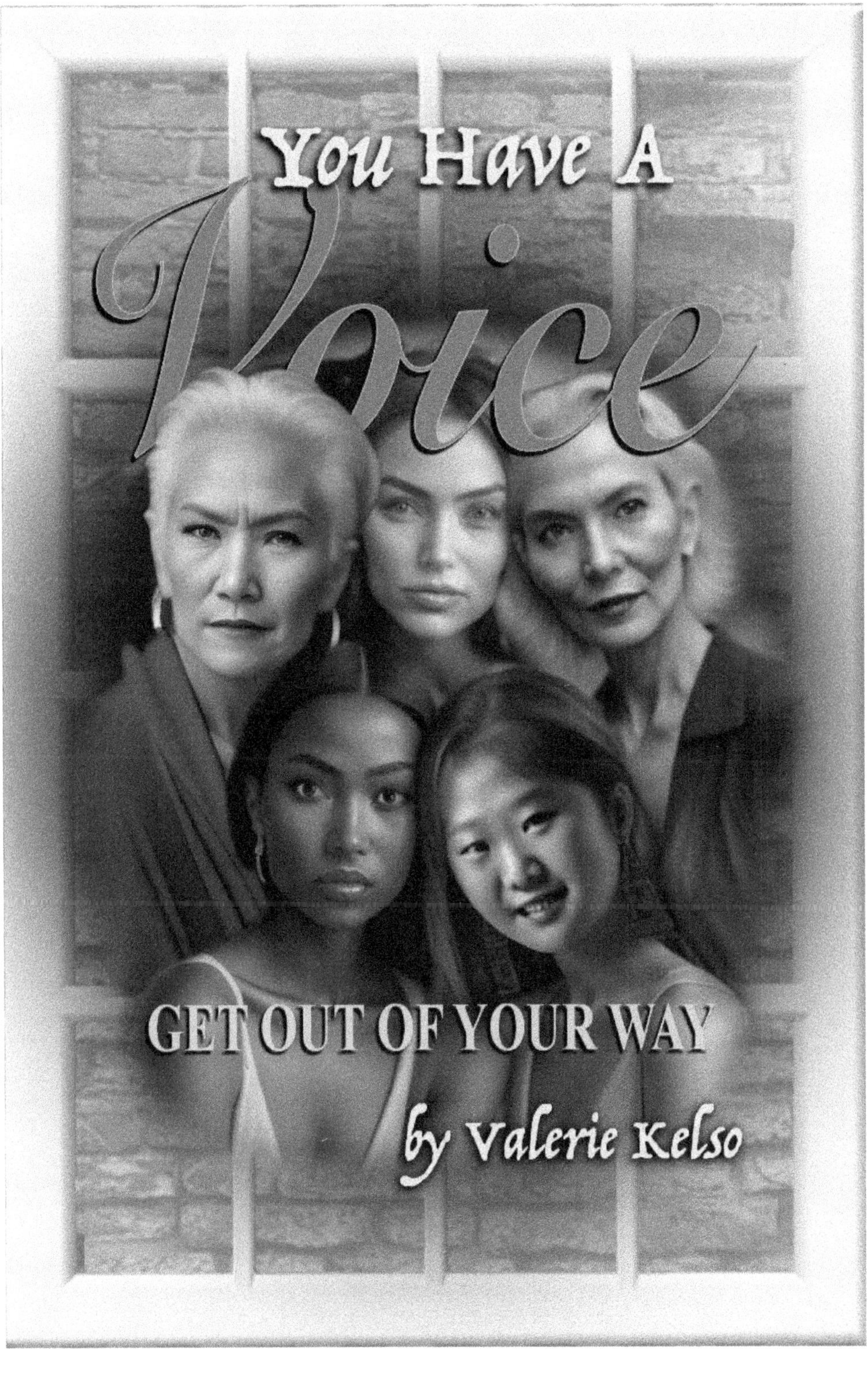
You Have A
Voice
GET OUT OF YOUR WAY
by Valerie Kelso

You Have a Voice, Get Out of Your Way
By Valerie Kelso

Cover Designed by Jazzy Kitty Publications
Published by Jazzy Kitty Publications
Logo Designed by Justin Ackerman
Editor: Anelda L. Attaway

© 2024 Valerie Kelso
ISBN 978-1-954425-95-8
Library of Congress Control Number: 2024903016

TABLE OF CONTENTS

TABLE OF CONTENTS

TABLE OF CONTENTS

INTRODUCTION

Valerie E. Kelso, originally from Birmingham, England and now living in Texas, is a remarkable woman on a mission to heal and empower those who have endured traumatic life experiences. As the owner of Purple Light Touch Foundation (PLTF), she has dedicated herself to supplying support and care to women and girls on their journey towards recovery.

Valerie's extensive ability and qualifications encompass a wide range of fields. She is a Professional Bodyologist, a Licensed Medical Massage Therapist, a Massage Instructor, a Mentor, a Speaker, an Advocate for women and girls facing abuse, a Social Philanthropist, and a Writer. In addition, Valerie serves as a community events coordinator and hosts a weekly podcast titled "Don't Believe the Hype Show Life." Through this platform, she aims to create a positive space for authors, activists, and advocates working against abuse. For more information, please go to www.purplelighttouchfoundation.org and www.dontbelievethehypeshow.life to visit the websites.

Valerie's own life has been marked by deep emotional scars, including the devastating loss of her daughter and enduring physical wounds from a knife attack. Weary of the relentless cycle of abuse, she reached a point where she contemplated ending her own life. Amidst her pain, Valerie persistently questioned God, seeking answers to the profound injustices she had experienced. "Why?" she asked. "Why did she have to endure the heartbreak of a stillborn baby? Why did her abusers continue to inflict pain and suffering?"

Yet, amidst the darkness, Valerie found a glimmer of hope. She felt a profound calling from a higher power, sensing that God had a grand purpose for her life. Her determination to survive grew stronger, and she recognized her potential as an advocate for women and young girls who had faced similar struggles.

In the following pages, we will delve into Valerie's extraordinary journey. From the depths of her own despair, she appeared as a beacon of light and resilience. Through the creation of the Purple Light Touch Foundation, she has become a catalyst for change, offering solace, healing, and empowerment to those who need it most. Join us as we explore Valerie's inspiring story and the transformative impact she continues to make in the lives of countless women and young girls. In 2001, I found myself standing in my kitchen, overwhelmed with frustration and despair. I cried out to God, questioning my purpose and expressing my belief that life was filled with suffering. At that moment, I received a surprising response from a higher power. God assured me that my life had a greater calling—to help people. This revelation puzzled me because I felt incapable of helping myself, let alone others. Filled with anger, I lashed out by throwing a teapot at my glass doors and fish tank, longing to hear something shatter just as I felt broken inside.

The catalyst for my outburst stemmed from a situation where I had warned someone about the dangers of taking part in drug trafficking. I received a divine message to share with this person, and I went to great lengths to help him change his plans and even provided him with the necessary items. Although he safely returned from his trip, he misconstrued my actions and believed I had supernatural abilities, leading him to try to burn down my house during a drug-induced episode.

Once again, God's intervention saved me. Weeks prior to this incident, I had met a peculiar situation where my car supposedly ran out of gas unexpectedly. Perplexed, I reached out to the person who lent me his gas can. Unbeknownst to me, this act of kindness and the presence of the gas can in my backyard played a crucial role in safeguarding my home and the lives of my grandchildren. When the individual looked to ignite a fire, he couldn't find the gas can, as it remained in my yard, unbeknownst to him.

During this tumultuous period, God revealed a plan for my future. Despite being on disability due to a work-related injury that caused excruciating pain in my lower back and right arm, I received divine instruction to buy my house and take out a mortgage for only ten years, as I would be moving in ten years. This directive seemed impossible, considering my financial circumstances and health condition. When I initially applied to buy a house, I faced rejection. Unbeknownst to me, this setback was a blessing in disguise, as the housing agency had plans to replace all the windows in the property with double-glazed ones, which would have incurred significant costs if I had already bought the house. Undeterred, I persevered and made a second attempt to buy a house. Miraculously, I was able to buy my property for just $24,000. Little did I know this would prove to be a wise investment. Eventually, when I decided to move from that house, I sold it quickly for $99,000, realizing a substantial return on my investment. This series of events showed God's unwavering presence and protection in my life. Through moments of despair, frustration, and unexpected challenges, I discovered that divine guidance and providence were at work. The journey was filled with hardship, but it also revealed God's ability to turn adversity into blessings and to supply a path forward, even in the face of seemingly insurmountable obstacles.

Chapter 1

Breaking the Chains: Dispelling Childhood Myths

Myths from childhood are persistent beliefs instilled in us from an early age, shaping our worldview as we transition into adulthood. These ingrained notions, often false and potentially harmful, demand confrontation to pave the way for personal healing and growth. Recognizing their impact, we embark on a journey to dismantle these myths and replace them with empowering truths.

Childhood myths, though seemingly innocuous, are not synonymous with reality. They can intertwine elements of truth with falsehood, creating a mental landscape marked by confusion and self-doubt. Challenging these ingrained beliefs becomes paramount to breaking free from a cycle of deception and fostering genuine personal development.

The process involves distinguishing between lies and truths, unraveling the intricacies of these myths that have taken root in our minds. Believing in falsehoods perpetuates mental turmoil, hindering the potential for self-assurance and growth. Embracing the truth becomes a transformative act, allowing us to reclaim power and establish a foundation built on authenticity.

As a guide on your journey, I am committed to helping you navigate through the complexities of childhood myths. Through healing practices and support, we aim to empower you to confront and dismantle these destructive beliefs. This journey is not about erasing your past but about reshaping your understanding of yourself, fostering resilience, and embracing a mindset grounded in truth.

Breaking free from the grip of childhood myths is a liberating endeavor. It involves unraveling the tangled web of misconceptions and embracing the inherent power of truth. It prompts reflection on why these myths persist, even when confronted with the undeniable reality. Is it easier to hold onto a comforting lie than to face the sometimes challenging truths of our experiences?

These myths may offer a semblance of comfort or familiarity, creating a protective cocoon around our beliefs. The process of dismantling them requires courage and a commitment to self-discovery. It involves understanding the roots of these myths, acknowledging their impact, and consciously choosing to embrace the truth, no matter how uncomfortable it may be.

In essence, breaking free from childhood myths is an act of self-liberation. It is a choice to embrace the authenticity of your experiences and challenge beliefs that no longer serve your growth. Through this process, you can cultivate resilience, foster genuine self-assurance, and embark on a journey toward authentic personal development.

Chapter 2

Can Time Truly Heal All Wounds?

We have all come across the popular saying, "Time will heal all wounds." It is a phrase often spoken to offer solace or encouragement. But when it comes to individuals who have experienced abuse, rape, neglect, or childhood trauma, time alone does not always bring healing. Instead, many of us learn to cope by burying our experiences deep inside and avoiding discussions about them. Unfortunately, this can lead to strained relationships, as friends and family may grow tired or struggle to understand the complex emotions we carry. Whether we choose to suppress our feelings or redirect our focus toward negativity, a lack of positive answers about our past can contribute to these patterns. Seeking professional help can be tremendously beneficial for our healing journey and overall well-being.

The purpose of this book is to show you that I have been where you are right now. Yes, I have experienced depression, abuse, suicidal thoughts, anger, and teenage motherhood. Do I still have lingering issues? Absolutely. Healing is an ongoing process that unfolds day by day. Today, I have my own business dedicated to helping others go through their traumatic life experiences. The question of whether time heals is a personal choice we each must make. Will we allow ourselves to remain stuck, or will we find the strength to rise again?

Consider yourself like a car. When the fuel is low, you are sure to fill it up because you know it will not go anywhere running on empty.

Similarly, when you are feeling depleted, it is crucial to find ways to recharge yourself. Engage in volunteer work, join a group that helps others, or develop a hobby that brings you joy. Through these self-care practices, you will gradually learn how to heal yourself, and over time, you will see improvements.

I vividly recall my teacher saying, "There is no such word as 'Can't': You Can," when I was 11 years old. It left an impression on me. In the same way, I want you to embrace the belief that you have the power to overcome obstacles and navigate your healing journey. This book aims to empower you, sharing my own experiences and supplying insights and guidance along the way. Remember, healing is a choice—one that begins with taking the first step toward a brighter future. Embarking on the journey of healing is a courageous choice—one that marks the first step toward a brighter and more hopeful future. While the path may seem daunting, it is essential to recognize that you have the strength within you to navigate it. Believe in yourself and your capacity for growth. Your story is not yours alone; by sharing it, you connect with others who have faced similar challenges. This interconnection reinforces the truth that you are not isolated in your experiences.

Choosing to heal can be intimidating, and acknowledging the need for healing requires vulnerability. This vulnerability is a strength—a declaration that you are ready to confront your wounds and transform them into sources of resilience. By taking the initiative to share your story, you not only validate your experiences but also create a space for others to do the same.

It's okay to be apprehensive about the healing journey. Healing often involves revisiting painful memories, unraveling deep-seated emotions, and challenging ingrained beliefs. But within these challenges lies the potential for growth, self-discovery, and liberation from the burdens of the past.

Believing in your ability to heal is fundamental. Trust that, despite the uncertainties, you have the inner strength to navigate the twists and turns of the healing process. Cultivate a mindset that acknowledges your worth and resilience. By doing so, you empower yourself to break free from the shackles of pain and step into a future defined by personal growth and well-being.

Sharing your story is not only an act of courage but also a powerful form of self-expression. It provides a voice to your experiences, allowing you to be seen and heard. In turn, this contributes to a collective narrative of strength, resilience, and the triumph of the human spirit over adversity. You become a beacon of inspiration for others who may be on a similar path. Remember, you are not alone. Countless individuals have embarked on healing journeys, facing challenges, uncertainties, and fears. By opening up about your experiences, you create a community where empathy and understanding thrive. This interconnectedness reinforces the shared strength found in vulnerability.

In summary, choosing to heal is a transformative decision that marks the beginning of a profound personal journey. Embrace the courage within you, believe in your capacity for growth, and share your story with the understanding that you are not alone. By doing so, you not only contribute to your healing but also inspire others to embark on their own paths toward wellness and resilience

Chapter 3

Embracing Emotions and Feelings

As a child, it was common for parents and loved ones to try to alleviate your sadness or pain by treating you to special things or taking you out for a meal. While their intentions were good, it is important to recognize that sometimes it is necessary to go through the hurt and pain together as a family and openly express your true emotions. Just as we have no problem expressing joy, it is equally important to be able to express sorrow and sadness.

It is crucial to communicate how you are truly feeling inside to your loved ones. However, sometimes, they may be unwilling or unable to listen because they may feel like they have failed you. In such cases, it is important to find someone you trust, such as a school counselor, teacher, or another supportive individual to talk to. Keeping feelings of sadness to yourself may be detrimental to your well-being, so it is essential to reach out and share all of your emotions with someone who can supply understanding and support.

Growing up, you may have experienced fear in showing your true feelings, as you feared being picked on or judged. This fear may have led you to follow what others said or wanted, causing anger and a lack of smiles. It is crucial to recognize the impact that suppressing your emotions can have on your overall well-being. By acknowledging your feelings and finding safe outlets to express them, you can begin to heal and regain a sense of authenticity and inner peace. Remember, it is okay to be vulnerable and share your emotions with trusted individuals who will support and understand you.

It is essential to acknowledge that your feelings are valid and real. No one has the right to dismiss or invalidate your emotions. Sometimes, we may feel the pressure to hide our true feelings because it does not align with societal expectations or the image we want to project. However, suppressing your emotions can have negative consequences and lead to a cascade of unresolved emotions, behaviors, and feelings that can manifest as various issues.

By not expressing your emotions, you deny yourself the opportunity to process and address them in a healthy way. Emotions are a natural part of being human, and allowing yourself to feel and express them is crucial for your well-being. Holding them in can lead to increased stress, anxiety, and even physical health problems. It is important to create a safe and supportive environment where you can freely share and express your emotions without fear of judgment or ridicule.

Remember that it takes courage and strength to acknowledge and communicate your feelings. Seeking support from trusted friends, family members, or mental health professionals can provide you with a listening ear, understanding, and guidance. By embracing your emotions and addressing them, you can embark on a path of healing, growth, and emotional well-being.

Chapter 4

Empower Yourself: Taking Ownership of Your Feelings

You are in control of your feelings, actions, and decisions. Nobody can force you to feel a certain way or act in a particular manner without your consent. It is crucial to recognize that you have the power to assert yourself and set boundaries to protect your emotional well-being.

Communication is the key when expressing your feelings effectively. No one can accurately read your mind or understand your emotions unless you openly express them. It is important to use clear and assertive communication, both verbally and non-verbally, to convey your emotions and needs to others. By doing so, you promote understanding and create opportunities for resolving conflicts and building healthier relationships.

It is understandable discomfort is not a pleasant feeling, and experiencing negative emotions like anger, depression, loneliness, anxiety, sadness, or fear can be challenging.

However, it is essential to take responsibility for your own actions and emotions rather than blaming others for how you feel. By taking ownership of your emotions, you empower yourself to make positive changes and seek support or professional help when needed.

When dealing with someone who has hurt you, it can be helpful to practice expressing your feelings in a safe and controlled environment. Standing in front of a mirror and rehearsing what you want to say can supply a sense of empowerment and clarity. Writing down your thoughts and feelings beforehand can also help organize your thoughts and ensure that your message is clear and effective.

Remember, you have the right to express your feelings, set boundaries, and take responsibility for your own emotional well-being. By doing so, you can assert your personal power and create healthier relationships with yourself and others.

Gaining Insight into Yourself

It's crucial to acknowledge the reality of the trauma you've experienced and firmly resist anyone attempting to diminish your inherent worth as a person.

Embrace openness about your experiences. Finding your voice is liberating, and there is no need to feel shame in sharing your story. Speaking out can be a powerful step toward healing. Reject the notion that you are alone in your journey. Understand that there are compassionate individuals ready to support you and guide you in recognizing your intrinsic value.

Redirect the emotional energy invested in hurtful situations. Instead of dwelling on past pain, channel that energy into pursuits that contribute to your personal growth and overall happiness.

Harness your emotional energy for positive change in your life. Rather than allowing it to be a source of distress, learn to utilize your emotions constructively, creating positive situations that enhance your well-being. By consciously directing your emotional energy, you empower yourself to shape a more fulfilling and positive life.

Chapter 5

Navigating My Own Healing Journey

Growing up in a large family setting, emotional experiences often took a backseat, as my mom was always pregnant, resulting in sibling rivalry. This environment instilled in me the habit of suppressing emotions and feelings. However, over time revealed the complexity of emotions, showcasing their potential to be misleading from reality.

Being distinct from my siblings made me susceptible to bullying and name-calling, fostering a profound sense of isolation. The solitude I experienced during this period laid the foundation for my involvement in multiple abusive relationships, as my self-worth was not fortified against external pressures. Transitioning into adulthood, my connection with God became a comforting refuge, serving as an imaginary friend during times of emotional turbulence.

It's a common reality that family and friends may remain oblivious to our emotional struggles, making it imperative to proactively share our feelings. Neglecting this vital aspect of communication can contribute to the development of depression and unwarranted negative thoughts and emotions.

Taking control of our emotions is a transformative and gradual process that necessitates cultivating self-love. This journey becomes especially crucial to avoid falling into the destructive patterns of abusive relationships. In the upcoming chapters, we will explore various strategies designed to help us assert control over our emotions and, concurrently, enhance our self-worth. By developing a robust sense of self and aligning with our core values, we fortify ourselves against the potential harm posed by detrimental relationships.

Understanding the emotional aspect of our existence, we embark on a journey of self-discovery and healing. It involves acknowledging the multifaceted nature of emotions and learning to navigate their complexities effectively. The process requires dismantling the ingrained habit of suppressing emotions and, instead, embracing a healthier approach to expressing and addressing them.

By fostering a profound sense of self-worth, we create a protective shield against the influences of abusive relationships. This involves recognizing our intrinsic value, irrespective of external judgments or mistreatment. Empowered by self-love and self-respect, we can cultivate an environment that promotes healthy connections and rejects toxic relationships.

In essence, my story underscores the transformative power of understanding and owning our emotions. Through self-love, self-discovery, and an unwavering commitment to cultivating a strong sense of self-worth, we can break free from the cycle of abusive relationships and pave the way for a more fulfilling and empowered life.

Chapter 6

"Reclaiming My Voice: From Silence to Liberation"

In the odyssey of my life, the recognition of possessing a voice emerged after enduring the weight of silence for years. Childhood echoes reverberated with admonitions to keep quiet, resulting in silent suffering through countless days and nights. Bullying, teasing, and name-calling cast shadows over my early years, both within the confines of home and the school environment. Despite a yearning to express myself, the fear of becoming a target silenced my voice.

As I transitioned into adulthood, I found myself ensnared in abusive relationships where asserting myself only fueled further mistreatment. My voice became muted, and I adopted a "yes person" to evade additional torment. Despite internal prompts urging me to speak out, fear held me captive. The pivotal year of 2018 marked my liberation from the shackles that had bound me.

Amid the trials of rebuilding my life post-homelessness, a shattered marriage, and depression, my sister's visit acted as a catalyst for transformative change. The confines of a cramped one-bedroom apartment amplified my struggles, and the overwhelming desire to join them intensified my pain. An airport confrontation with my sister became the crucible of liberation, where I, attempting to be a peacemaker, unwittingly paid a heavy price later in their visit.

In that heated exchange, I found my voice and unleashed a torrent of emotions long suppressed. For the first time, I articulated my feelings, addressing childhood wounds, harboring hatred, and the myriad emotions I had bottled up. The airport became my arena of freedom, and as I departed that night, I felt light, unburdened by anger and pain. It was a metamorphic experience, and I emerged anew, recognizing my strength as a woman, and embracing self-love. The airport, a symbolic weigh station, felt like a divine intervention, urging me to shed the excess weight and leave my baggage behind. I walked out a new woman, liberated from the past.

I learned that clutching onto past trauma only inflicts harm upon oneself, as the tormentors have often moved on. Suppressed trauma can manifest as physical illness, underlining the imperative need to release it. My journey illuminated the truth that no one should pilfer your voice; the power to break free from self-imposed inhibitions lies within. Embracing my voice empowered me to seize control of my destiny and live authentically.

Ask Yourself and Answer?

Understand that you need to take a step back and take a good look at yourself in the mirror. What do you see?

_____

_____

_____

_____

_____

_____

Have you ever asked yourself, "Why did I do that?"

_____

_____

_____

_____

_____

_____

_____

Do you second-guess yourself?

_____

_____

_____

_____

_____

_____

_____

We all do that, and it can mess with our emotions. Each night, I go
through my day asking what I could have done better. Was I productive?

_____

_____

_____

_____

_____

_____

_____

You need to know what you like or do not like and what is acceptable to you, and you have healthy boundaries. Are you happy-go-lucky? How will what you do affect others around you? Get to know you and why self-care is particularly important. No one can love you more than you can by loving yourself.

_____

_____

_____

_____

_____

_____

_____

_____

Chapter 7

The Six Steps to the Process of Recovery

Step One

Acknowledge the Presence of Trauma:

Take the first crucial step in your healing journey by acknowledging the presence of trauma in your life. Recognize that you may have experienced distressing events or circumstances that have left a lasting impact on your well-being. This acknowledgment is the foundation upon which you can build your path toward healing and resilience.

Understand and Come to Terms with Your Experience:

Delve into a process of understanding and coming to terms with the specific traumas you have faced. Reflect on the events or situations that have caused emotional pain or distress and allow yourself to comprehend the depth of their impact. Coming to terms with your experiences involves acknowledging the associated emotions and working towards acceptance, fostering a sense of empowerment over your narrative.

Embrace the Journey of Self-Discovery:

Recognizing and understanding trauma opens the door to a transformative journey of self-discovery. Explore the intricacies of your emotions, thoughts, and reactions in the aftermath of traumatic events. Embrace the process of unraveling the layers of your experiences, allowing for a deeper understanding of yourself and the ways in which trauma has shaped your perception of the world.

Seek Support and Professional Guidance:

While self-awareness is a powerful tool, seeking support is equally essential in the journey to recognize and address trauma. Reach out to friends, family, or mental health professionals who can offer understanding, empathy, and guidance. Professional support can provide valuable insights, coping mechanisms, and a safe space for processing emotions as you navigate the complexities of trauma.

Cultivate Resilience Through Healing Practices:

As you acknowledge and understand trauma, actively engage in healing practices that promote resilience. Explore therapeutic interventions, mindfulness techniques, or creative outlets that resonate with you. Cultivate a toolbox of coping strategies that empower you to navigate the challenges associated with trauma, fostering a resilient spirit that can withstand the impact of past experiences.

Summary: In summary, recognizing trauma involves the crucial steps of acknowledging its presence in your life and understanding the specific experiences that have shaped your journey. Embrace self-discovery, seek support, and actively engage in healing practices to foster resilience and empower yourself on the path to recovery.

Embracing Healing: Responding to the Pain of Trauma
Step Two

In the intricate landscape of healing from trauma, the ability to react to pain is a pivotal step toward reclaiming one's emotional well-being. This process involves acknowledging the presence of pain, allowing oneself to experience and process it, accepting a range of emotions, and uncovering any hidden feelings that may linger beneath the surface.

Allow Yourself to Experience and Process the Pain:

Grant yourself permission to traverse the depths of your emotions and confront the pain associated with the trauma. Suppressing or avoiding these feelings may hinder the healing process. Instead, create a safe space for acknowledging the pain, allowing it to surface and be felt. By giving yourself the time and permission to experience these emotions, you lay the groundwork for a more profound and authentic healing journey.

Find, Accept, and Express Your Emotions and Reactions:

In responding to the pain, actively seek to identify, accept, and express the spectrum of emotions and reactions tied to your traumatic experiences. Whether it's anger, sadness, fear, or confusion, acknowledging these emotions is a courageous act that can lead to greater self-understanding. Embrace the complexity of your emotional responses, recognizing that each emotion is a valid part of your healing process.

Uncover Any Hidden Emotions That May Be Lingering:

Beyond the surface-level emotions, delve into the recesses of your psyche to uncover any hidden feelings that may be lingering. Trauma has a way of burying emotions deep within, often as a survival mechanism. Bringing these hidden emotions to light requires patience and self-compassion. Journaling, therapy, or introspective practices can aid in uncovering these concealed emotions, allowing you to address them consciously.

Reacting to the pain is not about dwelling on negativity but acknowledging and understanding the emotional aftermath of trauma. This process fosters self-compassion, as it recognizes the validity of your feelings and allows you to release the emotional burden that trauma may have imposed.

Embrace Self-Compassion and Patience:

Reacting to pain necessitates the practice of self-compassion and patience. Understand that healing is a journey, and each step taken is a triumph in itself. Cultivate a supportive inner dialogue that acknowledges your strength and resilience. Patience becomes a guiding force as you navigate the ebbs and flows of the healing process, allowing for the gradual release of pain and the emergence of newfound strength.

Summary: In conclusion, reacting to the pain associated with trauma is an integral facet of the healing journey. By allowing oneself to experience and process the pain, finding, accepting, and expressing emotions, and uncovering hidden feelings, individuals can embark on a transformative path towards healing, self-discovery, and ultimately, reclaiming their sense of well-being.

Revisited: Recollecting and Re-experiencing Past Events
<u>Step Three</u>
In the pursuit of personal growth and emotional resilience, the act of recollecting and re-experiencing past events emerges as a

transformative journey. This process involves reviewing and remembering both historical events and current circumstances, approaching these memories with a realistic perspective, and revisiting the associated emotions to gain a new understanding and outlook.

Review and Remember the Past Events and Your Current Circumstances:

Initiate the journey of self-discovery by intentionally reviewing and remembering past events that have shaped your narrative. Simultaneously, take realist stock of your current circumstances to understand the intersection of past and present. This reflective stance serves as a foundation for comprehending the factors that have influenced your journey and contributed to your current state of being.

Approach These Memories with a Realistic Perspective: Navigate the terrain of recollection with a deliberate commitment to realism. Avoid idealization or distortion of past events, as this can cloud your understanding of your own growth and development. A realistic perspective allows for an honest assessment of the challenges faced, accomplishments achieved, and the impact of past experiences on your present self.

Revisit and Re-experience the Associated Emotions:

Delve into the emotional landscape of your memories, revisiting and re-experiencing the range of emotions tied to those events. Whether joy, sorrow, triumph, or challenge, each emotion is a thread woven into the fabric of your narrative. By embracing and acknowledging these emotions, you create space for a more authentic understanding of your past and present.

Gaining a New Understanding and Outlook:

As you re-experience these emotions, the transformative power lies in gaining a new understanding and outlook. This entails extracting valuable lessons from past experiences, recognizing personal growth, and identifying patterns that have contributed to your current circumstances. This newfound understanding becomes a compass that guides you toward intentional and informed decision-making in the future.

Recollecting and re-experiencing past events is not about dwelling in nostalgia or reliving moments unchanged. Instead, it is a deliberate and conscious effort to glean wisdom from the past, fostering personal growth and resilience. This journey enables individuals to appreciate the full spectrum of their experiences, embracing both challenges and triumphs as integral components of their unique narrative.

Summary: In summary, the process of recollecting and re-experiencing past events is a nuanced exploration of one's history and present circumstances. Approaching one's memories with a realistic perspective, revisiting associated emotions, and gaining a new understanding and outlook are key elements in this transformative journey toward self-discovery and resilience.

Recollect and Re-Experience:

- Review and remember the past events and your current circumstances.
- Approach these memories with a realistic perspective.

- Revisit and re-experience the associated emotions, gaining a new understanding and outlook.

Embracing Change: Readjusting to Move Forward
<u>**Step Four**</u>

In the pursuit of personal growth and healing, the pivotal act of readjusting serves as a transformative pathway. This involves reassessing and revising earlier assumptions and beliefs, fostering a new and healthier relationship with oneself, embracing innovative ways of living, and ultimately shaping a new identity that aligns harmoniously with one's growth and healing journey.

Reassess and Revise Your Earlier Assumptions and Beliefs:

Embarking on the journey of readjustment begins with a critical examination of earlier assumptions and beliefs. Assessing the validity and relevance of these pre-existing notions is essential for personal evolution. By questioning and, when necessary, revising these beliefs, individuals open themselves to the prospect of embracing new perspectives that better align with their current understanding and aspirations.

Develop a New and Healthier Relationship with Yourself:

Central to the process of readjusting is the development of a new and healthier relationship with oneself. This involves cultivating self-compassion, acknowledging personal strengths and areas for growth, and embracing a positive self-image. By fostering a compassionate and supportive internal dialogue, individuals pave the way for sustained personal development and resilience in the face of challenges.

Embrace New Ways of Living and Adapt to the Changes:

Readjusting necessitates a willingness to embrace new ways of living and adapt to the changes that come with personal growth. This may involve altering lifestyle choices, adopting healthier habits, or restructuring daily routines to align with evolving priorities. Embracing change becomes a cornerstone for navigating the transformative journey, fostering adaptability and a proactive approach to life's fluctuations.

Shape a New Identity that Aligns with Your Growth and Healing:

At the core of readjusting lies the process of shaping a new identity that authentically aligns with one's growth and healing. This entails integrating newfound insights, values, and aspirations into a cohesive sense of self. By actively participating in the construction of this evolving identity, individuals ensure that their self-concept aligns harmoniously with their journey toward healing and personal development.

Summary: In summary, readjusting to move forward is a dynamic and intentional process that involves reassessing beliefs, cultivating a healthier relationship with oneself, embracing change, and shaping a new identity aligned with growth and healing. This transformative journey empowers individuals to navigate life with resilience, adaptability, and an authentic sense of self.

Self-Revitalization: Reinvesting in Your Well-Being
Step Five
Amid life's demands and challenges, reinvesting in yourself

becomes a powerful and rejuvenating endeavor. This involves intentional actions aimed at enhancing your well-being, such as investing in self-care and self-compassion, treating yourself to moments of joy through new purchases or activities, and pursuing personal growth by exploring new interests or taking classes.

Invest in Self-Care and Self-Compassion:

At the heart of self-reinvestment is the commitment to self-care and self-compassion. Allocate time for activities that nourish your mind, body, and soul. Whether it's practicing mindfulness, engaging in physical exercise, or simply taking moments of quiet reflection, investing in self-care is a cornerstone for maintaining balance and resilience in the face of life's demands. Cultivate self-compassion by embracing your imperfections and treating yourself with kindness, recognizing that self-love is a crucial investment in overall well-being.

Treat Yourself to Joyful Moments:

Reinvesting in yourself involves indulging in moments of joy that uplift your spirits. Treat yourself by buying something new that brings you happiness or engaging in activities that spark joy and excitement. These intentional acts of self-indulgence serve as reminders of your worth and contribute to a positive mindset. Whether it's a small treat or a significant purchase, these moments of joy contribute to a more fulfilling and balanced life.

Pursue Personal Growth Through Exploration:

An essential aspect of self-reinvestment is the pursuit of personal growth. Take proactive steps to expand your horizons by exploring new interests or enrolling in classes that align with your passions. Embrace the opportunity for continuous learning and self-discovery. This commitment to personal growth not only fosters a sense of achievement but also enhances your overall well-being by keeping your mind engaged and curious.

Summary: In conclusion, "Self-Revitalization: Reinvesting in Your Well-Being" emphasizes the transformative power of intentional actions aimed at self-care, joy, and personal growth. By making deliberate investments in your well-being, you not only enhance your resilience but also contribute to a more fulfilling and balanced life.

Personal Reinvention: A Journey of Self-Investment
Step Six

Embarking on a journey of reinvention requires deliberate acts of self-investment, encompassing self-care, joyous indulgences, and a commitment to personal growth. This transformative process is not only about redirecting resources toward oneself but also about cultivating a mindset that prioritizes well-being and self-discovery.

Invest in Self-Care and Self-Compassion:

Central to the journey of self-reinvestment is the intentional allocation of time and energy towards self-care and self-compassion. Nurturing your mental and emotional well-being through practices like mindfulness, meditation, or therapeutic activities is an invaluable investment. Recognizing the importance of self-compassion involves treating yourself with kindness and understanding, acknowledging that it is okay to prioritize your needs, and taking a break when necessary. In the realm of personal reinvention, self-care is the cornerstone upon which resilience and balance are built.

Treat Yourself to Joyful Moments:

Reinvesting in yourself involves creating opportunities for joy and indulgence. Treating yourself can take various forms, from purchasing something new that brings you happiness to engaging in activities that spark joy and excitement. These intentional acts of self-indulgence are not mere luxuries but essential components of self-nourishment. They serve as reminders of your worth and contribute to an overall sense of fulfillment, making the journey of personal reinvention more rewarding.

Pursue Personal Growth Through Exploration:

Another crucial element of self-reinvestment is the pursuit of personal growth. This entails venturing beyond your comfort zone by taking classes or exploring new interests. Embracing the opportunity for continuous learning and self-discovery not only enhances your skill set but also broadens your perspective. Personal growth is a dynamic and ongoing process that aligns with the spirit of reinvention, opening doors to new possibilities and potential.

Summary: In essence, Personal Reinvention: A Journey of Self-Investment' encapsulates the transformative odyssey of intentional self-care, joyous indulgences, and continuous personal growth. By making conscious choices to reinvest in yourself, you embark on a path that not only revitalizes your well-being but also sets the stage for a more fulfilling and empowered life.

Chapter 8

Untangling Ties: Divorce Within the Family

Divorce is a challenging and often traumatic experience for everyone involved, especially the children. Unfortunately, parents may become so absorbed in their own conflicts and emotions that they do not realize the profound impact it has on their children. Instead of considering their child's well-being, they may inadvertently expect them to take sides in the battle, disregarding the fact that the child is a product of both parents' love and deserves to be shielded from such conflicts.

Children in divorce situations often find themselves caught in the middle, where their own feelings and needs are overlooked. They see their parents' constant arguments and may even be subjected to neglect as their parents focus solely on winning the battle, forgetting the toll it takes on the child's emotional well-being.

The absence of parental guidance during divorce can have devastating consequences for children. They may spiral into a staircase of depression, turn to substance abuse, or seek solace in destructive behaviors. When these children grow older and reflect on their experiences, they struggle to understand what went wrong. The truth is, it was their parents' inability to consider their feelings and prioritize their needs that contributed to their pain

Children should never be treated as pawns in a divorce. They were brought into this world through an act of love, and it is crucial to allow them to feel loved and supported despite the turmoil their parents are going through. Children deserve to be shielded from conflicts and allowed to keep a sense of stability, security, and unconditional love.

Parents need to step back from their own grievances and actively prioritize their children's emotional well-being during and after a divorce. This means supplying guidance, reassurance, and a safe space for children to express their feelings and fears. It also involves fostering a healthy co-parenting relationship, where both parents collaborate and communicate effectively for the sake of their child's best interests.

Divorce is undoubtedly challenging, but it is possible for parents to navigate this complicated process with compassion and empathy for their children. By putting aside their differences and focusing on their child's emotional needs, parents can supply the love and support necessary for their children to navigate this difficult transition and thrive in the face of adversity.

Silent Burdens: How Children Bear the Weight of Family Trauma

In many households, children are silently shouldering the weight of family trauma. They carry burdens and emotions that they are unable or unwilling to share with others, often resulting in feelings of anger and resentment. These unresolved issues can manifest themselves in negative ways, affecting not only the child's well-being but also their interactions with peers and their overall behavior. If you find yourself in such a situation, it is crucial to reach out and talk to someone as soon as possible.

Family trauma creates a domino effect, with the pain and distress rippling through the family dynamic. Without proper intervention and support, individuals who have experienced trauma may find themselves replicating the abusive behaviors they saw or endured. Unresolved emotions and unhealed wounds can lead to a cycle of perpetuating harm to others as individuals struggle to cope with their frustrations and do not take ownership of the triggers that drive their behavior.

It is vital to break this cycle by seeking help and talking to someone about your experiences. Speaking to a trusted adult, such as a teacher, counselor, or mentor, can supply a safe space to share your feelings and gain guidance on how to navigate the challenges you face; by opening and sharing your story, you can begin to unpack the weight you have been carrying and start the healing process.

Addressing family trauma requires a multifaceted approach. It involves recognizing and understanding the impact of the trauma, exploring the emotions it has evoked, and taking responsibility for one's actions and reactions. By seeking help, individuals can gain valuable insights into the root causes of their behaviors and develop healthier coping mechanisms.

By reaching out and talking about your experiences, you can begin to break free from the cycle of anger and resentment. It is important to acknowledge that your feelings are valid and that you have the power to choose a different path. Through therapy, support groups, or other resources available, you can embark on a journey of healing and personal growth, paving the way for a healthier and more fulfilling life.

Remember, it takes courage to confront family trauma and seek help, but doing so is a crucial step toward breaking the cycle and creating a brighter future for yourself and those around you. You deserve to live a life free from the burdens of the past and to forge meaningful connections based on understanding, empathy, and love.

To the children experiencing Their Parents' Divorce

I want you to know that the divorce your parents are going through is not your fault. It is important to understand that their decision to separate has nothing to do with you. When they brought you into this world, they did so out of love, and that love still exists, even if it feels distant or strained.

During this tough time, your parents may be caught up in their own emotions and conflicts. It can be confusing and hurtful to see them blaming each other or acting differently towards you. Remember, their actions reflect their struggles and not yours, but by dealing with the situation, they can forget how much they love you.

It is normal to feel a range of emotions during a divorce, including sadness, anger, confusion, or even guilt. Remember that it is okay to experience these feelings and that they do not define who you are as a person. Sometimes, it might seem like your family is falling apart, but the love your parents have for you is still constant, even if it is not always clear in their behavior.

You are not alone on this journey. Reach out to trusted family members, friends, or even a counselor who can supply support and guidance as you navigate these challenging circumstances. They can help you understand and process your emotions and offer reassurance that you are loved and valued.

Remember, divorce is a complex and complicated process for everyone involved, including your parents. They may be struggling to find their way through it. As they work through their own emotions, it is important to remind yourself that their love for you still exists, even if it might be temporarily overshadowed.

Stay strong and take care of yourself during this time. Surround yourself with people who uplift and support you. You are worthy of love, understanding, and happiness, regardless of your parent's current situation.

Chapter 9

Breaking the Silence: My Journey Through Domestic Abuse

Navigating the tumultuous waters of domestic violence at the tender age of 15, my story is a testament to the profound impact that a lack of love and a desperate yearning for acceptance can have on one's life. I found myself entangled in an abusive relationship, driven by societal pressures and a distorted perception of love.

The initial decision to be with this person was not rooted in genuine desire, but rather, it emerged from the constant narrative that I would never find another boyfriend. This misguided belief led me to settle for a relationship that soon resulted in an unplanned pregnancy, marking the inception of a turbulent journey.

Fear and loneliness became my constant companions. Living at home, I concealed the abuse from my family, creating a facade that shielded my suffering. However, when I moved into my apartment at the age of 18, the abuse escalated to unimaginable heights, culminating in the heartbreaking loss of my second child. The physical and emotional toll of those weeks and months was immeasurable, forever altering the trajectory of my life after that harrowing experience.

The severity of the abuse was such that even neighbors on lower floors could hear my cries and pleas for help from the sixth floor. This underscores the importance of open conversations with our children about the perils of staying in an abusive relationship. Silence is not the solution, as children can witness and internalize the trauma, influencing their future relationships.

Living in constant fear, I grappled with the debilitating cycle of denial and self-deception. The looming threat of another beating silenced my voice, and the persistent fear of saying or doing the wrong thing bound me to the shackles of abuse. I convinced myself that enduring this agony was a sacrifice worth making for the sake of my child. Unfortunately, my decision to stay had far-reaching consequences, as my daughter later found herself ensnared in an abusive relationship.

My plea to others facing similar circumstances is clear: Do not sacrifice your child's well-being by staying in an abusive relationship. It is vital to seek help, support, and resources to break free from the cycle of abuse. Taking a stand against such torment and prioritizing the safety and happiness of yourself and your children can pave the way for a healthier and brighter future. Remember, you are not alone; there are people and organizations ready to support you on your journey to healing and freedom.

In the aftermath of my harrowing experiences, I found strength in advocacy. As founder of the Purple Light Touch Foundation, I am committed to empowering women and young girls, providing them with resources, support, and a beacon of hope. My story is not just one of survival; it is a testament to the transformative power of breaking the silence and seeking help. Together, we can create a world free from the shadows of domestic abuse.

Empowering Yourself: Escaping Domestic Abuse and Rediscovering Your Worth

Breaking free from domestic abuse is not only possible but

essential for your well-being. The key lies in recognizing your own worth and understanding that staying in an abusive relationship is driven by fear, not love. Genuine love does not involve harm or hurt.

It's crucial to break the silence surrounding domestic abuse. Speak up and share your experience with someone you trust. You are not alone, and there is support available. Disregard the lies that claim no one will listen – your family cares, and there are people who want to help.

If you're a parent, consider the impact staying in an abusive relationship has on your child. Choosing to leave is a courageous step towards ending the cycle of misery and ensuring a safer environment for your child. Remember, no relationship is worth enduring abuse.

Self-care organizations exist to assist you on the journey to recovery. Reach out to them, seek support, and take the necessary steps to regain control of your life. Your well-being is paramount, and breaking free from domestic abuse is a powerful act of self-love and empowerment.

Chapter 10

Balancing Mental Health and Physical Well-Being

What do Mental and Physical health have in common? They are interconnected. If your mental health suffers, your physical well-being is likely to follow suit. For children, staying up all night to complete homework and spending excessive time on social media, comparing themselves to others can be detrimental in multiple ways. Lack of sleep affects daily functioning, while compromised diet choices tend towards quick and ready-made meals.

You may have come across the concept of Mind, Body, and Soul, which encompasses the three vital components of leading a healthy life. When you engage with others, it reduces the tendency to internalize emotions.

Mind: Nourishing your mind with positivity is essential as your thoughts shape who you become. A healthy mind positively influences your body.

Body: Engage in physical activities like walking and running, and adopt a healthy eating routine. Seek out activities that involve like-minded individuals, such as joining a book club, networking, or attending local events. Utilize the internet to discover nearby opportunities that may align with your interests or introduce you to new ones. This is a fantastic way to meet new people and discover new passions.

Soul: Connect with your spirituality and tap into the vastness of the universe. You can meditate while listening to soothing music and affirmations or engage in prayer. Keep yourself active by constantly learning something new.

When you keep a connection with all three aspects—mind, body, and soul—you will experience a significant improvement in your overall well-being. Daily life and living become more manageable, allowing you to navigate through each day with greater ease.

Chapter 11

Rediscovering Self-Worth and Finding Purpose in Helping Others

In times of trouble, it's easy to neglect oneself, especially when faced with challenges that disrupt sleep and appetite. The key is to break free from the weight of hurts, as unresolved pain can lead to lashing out and persistent anger. I understand this reality intimately, having experienced a profound loss – the passing of my second child, which triggered a downward spiral in my mental and physical well-being.

The trauma I faced at 18 years old during the painful experience of delivering a stillborn baby left an indelible mark on my psyche. Witnessing other parents with their children ignited a burning anger within me. The weight of the emotional burden affected not only my mental state but also took a toll on my physical health. Days and nights were spent in tears, shutting myself off in the confines of my two-bedroom apartment.

In the depths of despair, I questioned God, grappling with the injustice of the pain I was enduring. I wondered if I hadn't already gone through enough. Despite not conceiving again, I still had my daughter to care for. Determined to find purpose amid the grief, I chose to extend love and care to other people's children. This decision became a transformative step in my healing journey. By looking after the children of parents who, for various reasons, couldn't tend to their needs due to work, study, or other commitments, I discovered a newfound peace of mind and reclaimed a sense of self-worth. Turning my trauma into an opportunity to help others provided me with a lifeline. It served as a way to channel my grief into a positive force, helping not only those in need but also aiding my physical well-being and keeping me grounded. This act of caregiving became a source of motivation, giving me a reason to get up each day. It was a testament to the resilience of the human spirit – that even in the face of profound loss and heartache, there exists an innate capacity for compassion and a desire to make a positive impact in the lives of others.

In my story, the journey of healing involves turning personal pain into an avenue for connection, support, and understanding. It illustrates the power of finding purpose beyond one's struggles and using those experiences to empathize with and assist others in their time of need. Ultimately, my journey is a testament to the strength that comes from rediscovering self-worth and the healing potential found in acts of kindness and compassion toward others.

Chapter 12

From Homelessness: To Triumph

The prevalent myth surrounding homelessness often attributes it to issues of substance abuse, particularly alcohol and drugs. However, the reality is far more complex, with many individuals finding themselves without a home due to various life circumstances. Homelessness can be a consequence of trauma, such as abuse, illness, low income, or profound loss. It's crucial to recognize that every person experiencing homelessness deserves love and compassion, as their struggles may be rooted in circumstances beyond their control.

My personal journey into homelessness was a result of a tumultuous combination of factors orchestrated by my mother-in-law and exacerbated by my ex-husband's infidelity. The disbelief and despair I felt were overwhelming. Despite the challenges, God had other plans for me. Instead of returning to England, where my journey began, I found myself grappling with the harsh reality of homelessness in the parking lots of Walmart, WinCo's, and Albertsons.

Adapting to this new way of life, a dollar basin became my means of washing before starting a day's work. The invisible struggles of homelessness were masked as I maintained a facade of normalcy. Few knew about my predicament, and I spent countless nights crying in solitude. During this period, I even faced physical challenges like spraining my ankle, and with no access to a doctor, I relied on God-given skills to nurse myself back to health.

Despite the hardships, I refused to accept homelessness as my fate. I recognized that hitting rock bottom didn't mean surrendering to a life on the streets. I reminded God that I didn't leave England for this fate and that I believed He had a purpose for me. Massages became my lifeline as I utilized my skills to carve a path out of homelessness. The temporary struggle didn't define me; instead, it became a steppingstone toward a brighter future.

The message is clear: homelessness doesn't have to be a permanent state. I fought for myself, believing that I could break free from the cycle. It's a choice each individual facing homelessness can make – not allowing circumstances to define their identity. Putting God first and allowing His guidance to shape the path forward, I transformed my life.

Today, I am the proud owner of three companies – Purple Light Touch Foundation, PLT Massage and Wellness, and the Don't Believe the Hype Show. My journey stands as a testament to the power of resilience, faith, and the unwavering belief that homelessness doesn't define anyone. By choosing to fight for your potential and not letting circumstances dictate your destiny, you can break free from the cycle of homelessness.

Chapter 13

From My Depression to Light

Depression is a formidable struggle, a silent battle that often rages within the depths of one's soul. There were countless nights when I found myself lying in bed, questioning why life seemed to conspire against me. The weight on my shoulders was heavy, and I grappled with the uncertainty of whether I was truly experiencing depression. Tears stained my pillow as I faced name-calling and bullying, losing my voice in the process, yearning to vanish from a world that seemed overwhelmingly cruel.

The telltale signs of depression manifested in my daily life—eating became a challenge, motivation waned, and the thought of facing the outside world became an insurmountable task. Despite working as a childminder to feel useful and caring for the vulnerable, I wore dark-colored clothes as a metaphorical shield, believing myself to be ugly and unlike my siblings due to my tall, thin stature. The struggle reached a point where thoughts of ending my life became a haunting presence, the weight of continuing to live appearing unbearable.

In retrospect, I am grateful that I did not succumb to those thoughts, for it has allowed me to share my story with you today. Since those dark days, I have become a beacon of hope, making a positive impact on many lives. Depression and thoughts of suicide are profound and real, and it's crucial to acknowledge the validity of the emotions you are experiencing. The tears you shed now have the potential to be replaced by tears of joy in the future.

Today, I am blessed with a beautiful daughter and two wonderful granddaughters, and I wouldn't trade my world for anything. In moments of despair, consider the impact your absence would have on those you leave behind. Do you want them to endure the same suffering and depression? No, you don't. Reach out, find someone to talk to, and let your voice be heard. I spent countless nights hiding my inner thoughts behind a facade, but one day, I decided to fight back and discover my true self.

Embracing the reality that these emotions don't vanish overnight, I want you to know that you are a fighter, even if that strength isn't visible to you yet. You were placed on this Earth to be a source of light for others, so please do not extinguish your light prematurely. I didn't write this book for my own sake but with the hope that someone like you right now would find encouragement. I had you in mind while penning these words, with the desire that one day, you would say, "Ms. Valerie, thank you." Find something to do, immerse yourself in activities, and like me, you'll learn to control the reins of depression as you forge a path toward healing and self-discovery.

Chapter 14

Understanding and Supporting Suicide Awareness

Suicide Definition: the intentional taking of one's own life; destruction of one's interests or prospects: Buying that house was financial suicide.

Suicide Awareness Observations Risks:

- Family History of Suicide Attempts.

- Exposure to Violence.

- Impulsivity

- Aggressive or Disruptive Behavior.

- Access to Firearms.

- Being Bullied.

- Feelings of Hopelessness or Helplessness.

- Acute Loss or Rejection.

- Changes in Eating or Sleeping Habits.

- Frequent or Pervasive Sadness.

- Withdrawal from Friends, Family, and Regular Activities.

- Frequent Complains About Physical Symptoms, Often Related to Emotions Such as Stomachaches, Headaches, Fatigue, Etc.

- Decline In the Quality of Schoolwork.

- Preoccupation with Death and Dying.

Did you know that suicide rates are increasing, making it the second leading cause of death? Many of those who take their own lives have mental health issues, such as depression, or have been victims of bullying. Before someone reaches the point of suicide, they may have already made several attempts to seek help.

It is possible that you could be sitting next to someone right now who is contemplating suicide without even realizing it. It is crucial to be mindful of other people's feelings because you never know what they might be going through. Not everyone will look or act like you, and many individuals who consider suicide carry deep-seated pain and feelings of abandonment.

The impact of COVID-19 and the sense of loss has added more distress to our lives as the world we once knew no longer feels safe. I want you to understand that suicide should never be seen as a choice. If I had chosen to end my life when I hit rock bottom, I would not be here today, ready to help you navigate your own challenges. I had to consider the loved ones I would leave behind. Each day, I discovered that I was growing stronger. The feelings of depression and suicidal thoughts no longer consume me. I learned new coping mechanisms, such as finding a quiet space to lie down, practicing breathing techniques, writing, listening to empowering words or soothing music and seeking short motivational speeches on YouTube to prevent overwhelming my mind.

By shifting your mindset and reducing the focus on negative thoughts, you have the power to change. Negativity will always exist around you, but remember that you can rise above your thoughts and find a place of happiness

If you are someone who thrives in the company of others, be selective about the friends you surround yourself with and seek out positive role models.

Please reach out to someone you can talk to. Let your parents, school counselor, teachers, and friends know how you are feeling. If you notice any changes in the behavior of a depressed friend, be attentive. If you become aware of any child or adolescent expressing suicidal thoughts or discussing suicide, strongly encourage them to seek immediate evaluation from a trained and qualified mental health professional.

Chapter 15

My Journey of Faith and Resilience and Redemption

The decision to leave my comfortable and beautiful home and settle in an area that others couldn't comprehend appeared like madness to my family. They suspected my husband was taking advantage of me, unaware that God had a grand plan for my life, a plan known only to Him and me. Despite their doubts, my husband wasn't exploiting me; he was an instrument in God's design. In 2017, Jon decided to close the business, a revelation I will share in the true nature of my biography book.

Feeling like I hit rock bottom, a few weeks later, I found myself homeless with no family to turn to. The church, which I thought of as family, became strangers, and sores appeared under my armpits. Despair consumed me, and I felt forsaken by God. The weight of losing everything I had sacrificed for Him was overwhelming, leading me to contemplate suicide. Leaving behind a beautiful home in England only to end up with nothing felt like an unbearable pain.

Adding to the challenges, at the age of 52, Jon told me to leave the rented apartment, marking my second experience with homelessness in America. I continued to attend church, which concealed the depths of my despair from those around me. It was agonizing to witness my husband seemingly untouched by our dire circumstances.

Yet, in my darkest hour, God intervened once again. After sleeping in my car for a month, I cried out to Him, and miraculously, I found an apartment with no down payment needed—a testament to the faithfulness of the God I serve. From that point forward, my life took a positive turn. Despite having seemingly nothing left, I learned to trust in God, knowing that He had abundant blessings in store for me.

A turning point came when a client, coming in for a massage, handed me $360. Following God's prompting, I used the money to set up an LLC company on August 1, 2017. The remaining funds took care of my immediate needs. While many would have opted for a hotel room for a week, that $325 investment has kept me in business for over six years. I share my story to encourage others to reconsider their thoughts and place their trust in God, even when they feel they have nothing left. In those moments of emptiness, God has so much more to offer. My journey is a testament to His grace and provision, and I am now flourishing once again.

Chapter 16

A Closer Look at Human Trafficking/Prostitution

Sex Trafficking: is defined by the <u>Trafficking Victims Protection Act of 2000</u> as: "the recruitment, harboring, transportation, provision, or obtaining of a person for the purpose of a commercial sex act." It involves the use of force, fraud, or coercion to make a minor commit a commercial sex act. Sex trafficking is preventable. Understanding the shared risk and protective factors for violence can help us prevent sex trafficking from happening in the first place."

Teens get trafficked in so many ways. A quick test to see if you are being trafficked is that you are being **forced** (someone is physically forcing you), or you are being coerced (you are told that you owe a debt to them, so you must comply).

Signs of sex trafficking:

- Signs of Physical Abuse, such as Burn Marks, Bruises, or Cuts.

- Unexplained Absences from School/Class.

- Less Appropriately Dressed than Usual.

- Over Sexualized Behavior.

- Overly Tired in Class.

- Withdrawn, Depressed, Distracted, or "Checked Out."

- Brags about Making or Having lots of Money.

- New Tattoos of a Name, Symbol of Money or Barcode.

- The victim has an older boyfriend or new friends with a different lifestyle.

- Shows Signs of Gang Affiliation.

- Talks about Wild Parties and/or Invites Other Students to Attend Them.

Examples:

Let us say that you have a new friend & you think that he/she is a victim of trafficking. You may wonder why your friend would stay; there are lots of reasons, though they are not good ones:

- Your friend may have fallen in love with the trafficker.
- Your friend would rather do this than be back on the street.
- The trafficker may have threatened your friend's family or friends.
- The trafficker might have intimidated your friend so much they cannot see a way out.
- The "system" rejected your friend when they reached out for help.
- Your friend may be too embarrassed to admit they did not realize what was happening before it escalated.

Fictional Story

Kimberley, a 14-year-old girl from a broken home, experiences feelings of loneliness as her parents are often absent due to work commitments. During this vulnerable time, she meets Andy, a 19-year-old who offers her love and attention. Andy goes to great lengths to make Kimberley feel special, showering her with gifts and money. Unbeknownst to Kimberley, Andy is engaging in a process called grooming.

Kimberley finds herself caught in a dangerous situation with Andy. During an argument, Andy abruptly declares that their relationship is over, leaving Kimberley desperate to salvage what they had. Andy, aware of her emotional attachment, takes advantage of her vulnerability and tightens his grip on her.

Unaware of Andy's true intentions, Kimberley naively agrees to do anything he says, unknowingly stepping into a carefully laid trap. She is oblivious to Andy setting her up for a dangerous situation with potentially severe consequences. Now the trap is being set, she is in the trap of a sex trafficker. With the current trend girls are no longer being lured but taken.

It is a distressing reality that vulnerable individuals can be coerced and manipulated into engaging in criminal activities due to their desperation and lack of knowledge about the risks involved. This narrative emphasizes the importance of educating our children about the dangers of exploitation, coercion, and the tactics used by individuals looking to manipulate them.

If someone, regardless of their gender, shows an interest in you and starts showering you with gifts, it is important to exercise caution, Addressing the issue of exploitation requires collaborative efforts from various stakeholders, including educational institutions, law enforcement agencies, community organizations, and social services. It is vital to set up accessible resources, support systems, and intervention programs that can help by helping, counseling, and protection to individuals, enabling them to break free from the cycle of exploitation and rebuild their lives.

We aim to raise awareness about the tactics used by manipulators and emphasize the importance of early intervention, education, and support to prevent vulnerable individuals from falling victim to coercion and exploitation.

Falling Prey of Sex trafficking or Prostitution

It is a heartbreaking reality that many can fall victim to sex trafficking, often through manipulation and coercion by individuals they trust. It is crucial to raise awareness and educate young girls about the dangers and warning signs associated with sex trafficking to prevent them from becoming victims.

Kimberley's story highlights the tactics used by traffickers to exploit vulnerable individuals. Grooming, where a trafficker sets up trust and manipulates their victim emotionally, is a common method employed to lure young girls into the world of sex trafficking. They may shower the victim with gifts, attention, and false promises of love and security. Once trapped, the trafficker exercises control through threats, violence, and escalating debts.

Recognizing the warning signs and understanding the risks are essential for young girls. It is crucial to be cautious when entering relationships with older individuals who show excessive interest and supply gifts or money. If something seems too good to be true, it often is. Trusting one's instincts and being skeptical can help avoid dangerous situations.

Open communication with trusted adults is vital. Young girls should feel comfortable discussing their relationships and concerns with parents, guardians, teachers, or other responsible adults. Building a dedicated support network can supply guidance and protection.

Education on the tactics used by traffickers and the consequences of sex trafficking is key. Schools, community organizations, and parents can play a significant role in raising awareness among young girls. Teaching them about healthy relationships, setting boundaries, and recognizing signs of exploitation can empower them to make informed choices and protect themselves.

It is important to highlight that sex trafficking can involve not only men but also women and other teenage girls and boys acting as recruiters or traffickers.

Frequently, we overlook the signs of sex trafficking, often missing the telltale signs. Many teenagers appear older than they truly are, leading us to overlook the issue right in front of us.

During my childhood, our church stood across from the red light district, where women lingered day and night, engaged in what we then called prostitution. We observed pimps dropping off these women in flashy cars, adorned with fur or leather coats and dripping in gold.

Unlike today, back then, these women would return home at night, rather than being held captive. Over time, trafficking individuals became more profitable than dealing drugs, as they could be exploited repeatedly. Unfortunately, there's now a growing demand for younger victims.

I once attended a task force meeting where a state representative disparaged the massage profession. When I suggested simple solutions to address trafficking, he expressed interest but never followed through on our conversation. It raises questions about whether there are ulterior motives at play.

It's disheartening to see Amber Alerts and films like "The Sound of Freedom" treated as if trafficking isn't a significant issue. It's a pervasive problem across states and countries that we often sweep under the rug.

Victims of trafficking often struggle to break free due to fear, attachment to their abuser, or manipulation disguised as affection. Despite frequent Amber Alerts, we tend to disregard them if they're from another city, yet the victim could be right beside us in a fast-food restaurant, having been moved across the country

Prevention programs, support services, and resources should be made readily available to young girls who may be at risk or have already experienced exploitation. These services can offer protection, counseling, and help in breaking free from the cycle of trafficking.

Together, through awareness, education, and support, we can work towards protecting young girls from falling victim to sex trafficking and creating a safer environment for them to grow and thrive.

How Do I Help My Friend?

Listen

Make sure the know this is **Not okay** and is **Not love!**

Find out who they could go to for help and share that information.

Be a friend – **do not judge.**

Be patient, it may take some time for her to get the courage to act.

Can Someone Break Free from This Life?

Yes! There is help. You do not have to stay. Trafficking is not only wrong, but it is illegal. Even if you are selling yourself for sex, it is not your fault! To get out, you CAN tell a trusted adult or police officer, or you can call 1-888-373-7888.

Chapter 17

Overcoming Drug Abuse and Rediscovering Life

Drug Abuse: is a chronic disease characterized by looking for and using drugs. Addiction is compulsive and difficult to control despite harmful consequences.

Signs of Drug Abuse:

- Continuing to take a drug after it is no longer needed for a medical condition.
- Needing more of a drug to get the same effect.
- Inability to stop taking the drug, even when really wanting to.
- Spending a lot of time thinking about the drug – how to get more, when you will take it, how good you will feel, etc.
- Loss of interest in things you once liked to do.
- Borrowing money, you never pay back, or stealing to get more drugs.

You never know what you are getting into when you start dabbling with drugs. You may think it is harmless because it seems cool smoking a little bit of weed; however, it never stays there. You will be introduced to something much stronger, and before you know it, you are popping pills, taking heroin, or even meth. Your family, which was already broken, is now in turmoil. Your schoolwork will suffer, and you may end up dropping out of school. Your hair, skin, and personality will change. You may feel everyone is picking on you. Please do not think you are invincible and that you are going to be in control. The only person in control is the drug pusher because he knows you will be coming back repeatedly.

1. Before you decide to walk down this roadway, up your options.
2. Why are you feeling the way you do?
3. Have you thought about talking to someone?
4. Are you doing it because you see others doing it?
5. What's the consequence if you go down this road?
6. Do you think you can achieve a different outcome from others who have gone down this road, or will your outcome be the same?
7. What impact will it have on your family and friends?
8. What impact will it have on your future?
9. Do you know someone who has died from a drug overdose?
10. Write down your feelings.

Chapter 18

Love, Loss, and Liberation

At 18 years old, I faced a daunting reality when I discovered that my boyfriend harbored a deep love for smoking weed. Despite my reservations, fear led me to let him move into my apartment, driven by the desire for my child to have her father present. Little did I know that this decision would plunge me into a tumultuous journey.

Wanting to expand our family, I endured the pain of losing a child due to his actions. Every Monday, the routine trip to the post office for child allowance became a distressing episode. Instead of using the money for our family's well-being, I was compelled to hand it over to feed his drug habit or settle his debts. Living with a drug user and abuser took a toll on my finances, leaving me struggling to meet my daughter's needs.

Facing financial hardships, I became adept at stretching every dollar, mastering the art of preparing meals on a tight budget. The weight of my boyfriend's unpredictable moods and actions pressed heavily on me. Out of fear, I yielded to his demands, sacrificing my well-being and happiness. Forced to engage in illegal activities like separating and packaging cannabis for his sales, I endured this toxic cycle for years until I summoned the courage to walk away after he nearly took my life.

No one should endure this harmful and abusive environment. For those in similar situations, reclaiming control of life is paramount.

<u>Steps to Reclaim Control</u>:

- **Seek Support**: Reach out to trusted friends, family, or professionals who can provide guidance and support. Their advice and connections to resources can be instrumental in navigating through tough times.

- **Establish Boundaries**: Set clear boundaries with your partner and communicate your needs. Prioritize your safety and the well-being of your child as top priorities.

- **Seek Professional Help**: Consider seeking assistance from therapists, counselors, or support groups specializing in addiction and domestic abuse. They offer tools to cope with the challenges faced.

- **Access Community Resources**: Research local organizations offering support for individuals in similar situations. They may provide housing assistance, financial aid, legal advice, or other forms of support.

- **Focus on Self-Care**: Prioritize your well-being by engaging in activities that bring joy, practicing self-care routines, and surrounding yourself with positive influences. Breaking free from toxic relationships is a journey toward reclaiming your own narrative and building a life filled with self-love and empowerment. Remember, you have the strength and resilience to overcome these difficulties. By seeking help and making decisions that prioritize your safety and the well-being of your child, you can create a healthier and happier future for both of you.

Journal

Chapter 19

Understanding and Addressing Alcohol Abuse

Alcohol abuse is the habitual misuse of alcoholic beverage consumption.

Signs of Alcohol Abuse:

- An uncontrollable urge to drink.

- Lack of control over how much you drink.

- Negative thoughts when you are not drinking alcohol.

- You cannot relax or fall asleep without drinking.

- You need a drink in the morning to get going.

- To be social, you must drink.

- Alcohol serves as your escape from feelings.

- After drinking, you drive.

- You mix alcohol and medications.

- You drink when you are pregnant or caring for small children.

- When loved ones ask how much you drink, you do not tell the truth.

- You hurt people or become angry when you drink.

- It is tough for you to remember what you did when you were drinking.

- Your responsibilities suffer because of your drinking.

- Drinking has caused you legal problems.

- You tried to stop drinking but failed.

Perils of Early Alcohol Exposure and Embracing Resilience

It is not uncommon for well-meaning relatives to offer minors their first alcoholic beverage during holidays or gatherings. While seemingly innocent, this early exposure can have detrimental effects, potentially leading to a future struggle with alcoholism. The argument that "one sip won't harm you" holds little weight, as that single sip can pave the way for a destructive drinking habit. Despite the inclination to blame external factors, such as friends or peers, it is imperative for parents to acknowledge the significant role they play in shaping their child's relationship with alcohol.

Falling into the trap of alcohol abuse not only jeopardizes one's future success but also strains relationships, jeopardizes employment, and diminishes self-esteem. Even in the face of trauma, turning to alcohol is not a solution; instead, redirect negative energy into positive pursuits. It's crucial to recognize the power each individual possesses to be a positive force, transforming negativity into light.

When tempted to reach for the bottle, one must consciously choose to set it down and become a guiding light, not just for oneself but for others as well. Reflecting on my own life, I encountered challenges that could have led me down the path of alcohol or drug dependence. However, I made a deliberate choice not to let those experiences define me negatively. Opting to be in control of my destiny, fully aware of my choices, I now share the importance of resilience.

Being a victim of circumstances is not inevitable. Nobody wishes to endure bullying or life's traumas, yet standing up and proclaiming, "Not on my watch! I will be the beacon of light in the room. I will make a difference today," empowers individuals to rise above adversity. Many resort to drinking to mask the pain of trauma, believing it can drown their sorrows. Seeking help, talking to someone, admitting the existence of a problem, and changing the circle of friends are vital steps to break the cycle of alcoholism. Learning to say no, particularly when faced with demands for money, becomes a crucial aspect of denying support to an addict.

Embracing resilience entails acknowledging that challenges do not define us but shape us into individuals capable of overcoming adversity. By choosing to be the positive light in the lives of others, we break free from the destructive cycle of alcoholism. Each day presents an opportunity to make a difference, foster positive change, and inspire those around us to reject the lure of the bottle in favor of a brighter, more fulfilling future.

Alcohol and Resentment:

A Journey of Healing and Empathy

In the years 2017 and 2018, my life intersected with that of a remarkable young woman who became an invaluable pillar of support in my journey of rebuilding. She transcended the boundaries of friendship, evolving into a sisterly figure who, during moments of overwhelming hurt and pain, gently encouraged me with the words, "Not today, Ms. Kelso." In her presence, I found a safe haven to express my struggles.

Little did I know, behind her supportive facade, she grappled with her own demons of alcoholism and profound resentment rooted in a troubled marriage. She entrusted me with her traumatic experiences, laying bare her painful history of sexual assault and the emotional toll it exacted. We both carried the burdens of brokenness, yearning for solace and healing.

The true depth of her internal turmoil became glaringly apparent when I received a distressing call from her mother, revealing her attempted suicide. Unjustly, I found myself blamed for her desperate act, a moment when I wished to defend myself and redirect the blame towards her family, who failed to provide the necessary support. Despite our relatively brief connection, she had shared her family's secrets with me, exposing the underlying issues they had overlooked. Facing her own pain and trauma seemed an insurmountable task, and she wasn't prepared for the journey.

Encountering the Purple Light Touch Foundation and its mission resurfaced old wounds, emphasizing the importance of finding healing after trauma. Many remain unaware that the body and mind harbor past traumas, often manifesting as physical pain. I am grateful our foundation serves as a safe space for women who have endured past hurts.

This heart-wrenching experience illuminated the hidden struggles of functional alcoholics, where demons and spirits emerge behind closed doors as they attempt to drown their pain in alcohol. While my companion sought solace in drunkenness, I implored her, and others like her, to release the bottle and seek comfort in the Holy Spirit. True and lasting healing, transformation, and empowerment come through a genuine connection with the divine.

In sharing this story, my intention is to underscore the significance of self-reflection, understanding, and seeking help. Blaming others for our downward spirals perpetuates the cycle of pain and suffering. Instead, let us find the strength to confront our demons, lean on our faith, and foster an environment of empathy and support for those battling their internal struggles. Seeking help is not a sign of weakness but a courageous step towards healing and reclaiming one's life.

"LOOK IN THE MIRROR!"

Look in the mirror; what do you see?
I see my mother crying out for me.

Look in the mirror; what do you see?
I see my friends and family looking back at me.

Look in the mirror; what do you see?

Ok!

I am stealing from my friends and family.

Look in the mirror; what do you see?
I see me shoplifting, handcuffs waiting for me.

Look in the mirror; what do you see?
I am not the same person I used to be.

Look in the mirror; what do you see?
I see a face giggling with glee.

Look in the mirror; what do you see?
I see a junkie staring back at me.

Look in the mirror; what do you see?

I see myself: Is that me?

Look in the mirror; what do you see?

I see them pumping drugs out of me.

Look in the Mirror; what do you see?

I am looking! Keep looking; what do you see?!

NOOOOO!

All I SEE IS DEATH WAITING FOR ME!"

Chapter 20

The Menace of Stalking

Stalking: can include following, spying, watching, or otherwise harassing the victim, showing up at the victim's home or work, sending unwanted gifts, collecting information, making phone calls, leaving written messages, or appearing at a person's home or workplace uninvited. These acts individually are typically legal, but any of these behaviors done continuously results in committing the crime of stalking.

Signs of Stalking:

- Hang-up Calls and Messages from Unknown Contacts.
- The stalker is always driving by your house or job.
- The stalker obtains info on you before you provide it.
- The stalker uses gifts to make up for obsessive behavior.
- The stalker seems to have a "sixth sense" about when you leave.
- The stalker damages property and threatens you.
- The stalker attacks your reputation.
- The stalker leaves unwanted items or presents or flowers.
- Stalkers wait at places for a current/former partner.
- Stalkers send unwanted emails, or letters.
- Stalkers persistently post information, and spread rumors about a current/ former partner on the internet, in public places, or by word of mouth.

If you believe you are being stalked, it is crucial to take immediate action by reporting it, as some instances of stalking can escalate to life-threatening situations. Contact the police and inform someone about your whereabouts and who you will be with when leaving your home. Consider obtaining pepper spray for self-defense, as it can incapacitate your stalker, giving you an opportunity to escape. Raise your voice and scream loudly or carry a siren that emits a piercing sound. Often, the stalker will feel threatened and may flee.

When visiting unfamiliar places, take photographs of your parked car and share them with a trusted friend or family member. Keep your car keys readily accessible when returning to your vehicle. Never, under any circumstances, open the door for a stranger or exit your car if something seems amiss.

Prioritize finding a safe location where others can see you if you meet any issues with your vehicle, such as a flat tire. Remember, a wheel can be replaced, but your life cannot. Stay aware of your surroundings as it can potentially save your life. If you feel uneasy or threatened at any time, remain where you are and dial 911 at once. Remember, it is better to prevent a dangerous situation than to risk not making it back home safely.

Silent Shadows: My Harrowing Stalking Experience and the Journey to Empowerment

In the tumultuous years of 2016 and 2017, I found myself thrust back into the haunting nightmare of being stalked, an ordeal I had previously endured. What unfolded during this time was a disturbing revelation—an unwelcome tracker discreetly placed in my car by none other than my ex-husband, resuming his malicious actions. The unsettling incident occurred at a women's conference, where he persistently lingered around me, attempting to gain access to my car. A compelling inner voice urged me to check the back of my car, unveiling the undeniable evidence of a tracker. To this day, I hold onto that device as a chilling reminder of the invasion of my privacy.

As the chapters of 2017 and 2018 unfolded, the stalking persisted despite our separation. Driven by jealousy and insecurity, my ex-husband continued to monitor my every move, despite his own history of infidelity. Phone calls, unannounced appearances at my apartment and workplace, and even mail sent to my residence became routine tactics. Seeking help, I confided in our pastor about his distressing behavior, especially considering he had already remarried and ostensibly moved on.

The experience of being stalked is undeniably terrifying, particularly when faced alone and isolated. Walking away from him was an unexpected move on my part, and finding a new apartment was shrouded in fear fueled by the haunting stories he shared about his treatment of his first wife. Importantly, this narrative emphasizes that stalking doesn't always originate from strangers. The repercussions of his actions even infiltrated my workplace, causing discomfort among staff and resulting in a loss of personnel.

To prevent triggering his dangerous behavior, I have been compelled to limit my movements, meticulously selecting where I go. This harrowing tale underscores the deeply traumatic impact of stalking, an ordeal perpetrated by someone intimately known to the victim. It serves as a poignant reminder for individuals to recognize the signs, seek support from trusted allies, and take necessary precautions to ensure personal safety. No one should endure the fear and torment inflicted by a stalker.

By sharing this story, I aim to shine a light on the issue of stalking, fostering awareness and understanding. Moreover, it emphasizes the importance of learning self-defense, recognizing that a stalker's behavior can escalate to violence. Empowerment is not just about breaking free from the clutches of a stalker but also about arming oneself with the tools to protect against potential harm. Together, we can work towards creating a safer and more compassionate society, where the shadows of silent torment are dispelled, and victims find strength in their journey to empowerment.

Chapter 21

Shedding the Light on Cyberstalking

Cyberstalking: refers to repeated emails or online activity that inflicts substantial emotional distress on the recipient.

Signs of Cyberstalking:

- The cyberstalker is aggressively following you on social media platforms.
- They constantly text/email multiple times a day.
- They seem to always show up where you are using your phone's GPS.
- They try to contact you via any communication method available to them.
- They pretend to be someone you know to get personal information about you.
- They follow your family and/or friends either in person, on social media, or both.

In today's interconnected world, where we rely on the internet for various aspects of our lives, the issue of cyber stalking has become increasingly prevalent. As we actively engage with platforms like TikTok, Instagram, and Snapchat, it is essential to exercise caution to avoid becoming victims of cyberbullying or stalking. The information we choose to share online, whether it be personal pictures, details about our lives, or our interactions with others, can inadvertently attract unwanted attention and potentially lead to harmful consequences.

Social media platforms have supplied a virtual space for people to connect, share, and express themselves. However, these same platforms can also serve as hunting grounds for individuals with malicious intent. Teens are vulnerable targets for cyberstalking due to their active presence on platforms like TikTok, Instagram, and Snapchat. It is crucial for young users to be mindful of the content they post and the personal information they show.

One generic form of cyberstalking is catfishing, where individuals create fake identities to deceive and manipulate others online. This can lead to real emotional distress, as unsuspecting victims may form deep connections with someone who is not who they claim to be. By keeping a vigilant approach and being cautious about accepting friend requests or engaging in private conversations with unknown individuals, we can reduce the risk of falling victim to such deceitful practices.

Moreover, sharing intimate pictures or sensitive information online can have serious repercussions. Once something is posted on the internet, it can quickly spread beyond our control and fall into the hands of those with malicious intent. This can not only result in personal embarrassment but also make us vulnerable to threats, blackmail, or unwelcome advances. Therefore, it is crucial to think twice before sharing any content that may compromise our privacy or personal safety.

Additionally, cyberbullying is a distressing consequence of online interactions. Hurtful comments, rumors, and malicious messages can have a profound impact on one's mental and emotional well-being. The anonymity afforded by the internet can embolden bullies, making it vital for individuals to be aware of the signs of cyberbullying and seek support if they become victims. Reporting abusive behavior and reaching out to trusted friends, family members, or authorities can help combat the negative effects of cyberbullying. To protect ourselves from cyberstalking, it is essential to adopt certain safety measures.

Primarily, we must be mindful of the information we share online, ensuring that our privacy settings are properly configured. Regularly reviewing and updating our online profiles can help limit the amount of personal information available to potential stalkers. Additionally, we should exercise caution when interacting with strangers online and refrain from sharing sensitive information or engaging in risky behavior.

Education and awareness play a vital role in preventing cyberstalking. Schools, parents, and online platforms themselves must prioritize teaching young individuals about digital safety and responsible online behavior. Encouraging conversations about the potential dangers of the internet and fostering a supportive environment where victims can seek help without fear of judgment is crucial.

In conclusion, the internet has revolutionized the way we connect and communicate, but it has also brought about new risks, such as cyberstalking. By being cautious about the content we share online, adopting privacy measures, and promoting digital safety education, we can navigate the online world more securely and reduce the risk of falling victim to cyberbullying or stalking. Remember, protecting ourselves and our online presence is key to supporting a safe and positive online experience.

Chapter 22

Confronting Bullying

Bullying, characterized by the use of superior strength or influence to intimidate someone, remains a pervasive issue affecting individuals across various age groups. Whether it originates from siblings, parents, or peers at school, the impact of bullying on one's well-being cannot be underestimated. Unfortunately, many children enduring bullying suffer in silence, concealing their experiences due to the overwhelming fear of harm. Tragically, some even contemplate or carry out suicide. In the face of such adversity, it is crucial for victims to reach out, confide in someone, and recognize the value their lives hold.

Recognizing the Signs of Bullying:

- Unexplained injuries.
- Lost or destroyed personal belongings.
- Frequent headaches, stomach aches, or faking sickness.
- Changes in eating habits, such as skipping meals or binge eating.
- Difficulty sleeping or frequent nightmares.
- Declining grades, loss of interest in schoolwork, or reluctance to attend school.
- Sudden loss of friends or avoidance of social situations.
- Feelings of helplessness or decreased self-esteem.
- Self-destructive behaviors, such as running away, self-harm, or discussing suicide.

<u>Identifying Signs that a Child Is Bullying Others</u>:

- Frequent involvement in physical or verbal fights.
- Association with friends who bully others.
- Increasingly aggressive behavior.
- Regular visits to the principal's office or detention.
- Possession of unexplained extra money or new belongings.
- Tendency to blame others for their problems.
- Refusal to accept responsibility for their actions.
- Competitive nature and concern about reputation or popularity.

The impact of bullying extends beyond the immediate physical or verbal abuse, affecting the mental and emotional well-being of individuals. Children, in particular, may face challenges in expressing their experiences, making it essential to create a safe space where they can share their struggles without fear of judgment or retaliation.

It is crucial to raise awareness about the far-reaching consequences of bullying and foster an environment where victims feel empowered to seek help. Every life holds immense value, and no one should endure the stripping away of joy or the robbing of the life they deserve. By confronting the shadows of bullying and offering support, we can collectively work towards creating a compassionate society where kindness prevails over cruelty and every individual is treated with dignity and respect.

Healing from Bullying

Bullying is a haunting experience that can leave deep scars, instilling fear, and despair. I intimately understand this pain, as I navigated through the shadows of bullying during my own childhood. In the early years of senior school, I found myself subjected to mistreatment by several boys, creating an environment that made me dread going to school. In a desperate attempt to appease my bullies, I resorted to stealing sweets from the store, hoping it would put an end to the torment. The memories of those dark days linger—the tears, the overwhelming despair, and the haunting contemplation of ending my own life at the age of 11 years old.

Reflecting on the incredible journey I've undertaken since then, it becomes evident that succumbing to that despair would have deprived me of the chance to connect with others, to extend a hand of understanding and empathy. This book is a testament to my belief that everyone deserves compassion and support on their path to healing.

In later years, I discovered that the boys who bullied me actually harbored feelings for me and didn't want their friends to date me. Ironically, they began referring to me as "Sister Val." It was a revelation that added complexity to the layers of my experience.

I implore you, with all the sincerity in my heart, to break the silence and reach out to someone you trust. Speak to a counselor, confide in a friend, or seek guidance from a reliable adult. You don't have to face this alone. Your experiences and emotions are valid, and sharing your burden with someone offering support can be a powerful source of strength.

You are cherished and valued, even though it may be challenging to recognize during moments of pain and turmoil. Your unique purpose and worth extend far beyond the hurt inflicted by bullies. Your voice matters, and together, we can reclaim it. By speaking up and seeking help, you can regain control over your life and begin to heal the wounds that have caused so much anguish.

I understand the anger and frustration that can arise from feeling powerless to stand up for oneself. Please know that you are not to blame for the bullying you've endured. It is the bullies who should be held accountable for their actions. Your strength lies not in stooping to their level but in rising above hatred and cruelty, refusing to let it define you.

Find solace in the knowledge that you are not alone. Countless others have faced similar struggles, and together, we can create a network of support and understanding. You deserve to experience joy, love, and fulfillment. By reaching out, you take the first step toward reclaiming your happiness and embracing a future free from the shackles of bullying.

Hold on to hope, for brighter days await. Your journey to healing begins with a simple act of courage—reaching out for help. Trust in your resilience and know that there are people deeply invested in your well-being. You are not alone in this battle, and together, we can overcome the pain inflicted by bullying, paving the way for a brighter, more compassionate future.

Chapter 23

Dyslexia: Breaking Stigmas, Seeking Help, and Achieving Success

Dyslexia: A general term for disorders that involves difficulty in learning to read or interpret words, letters, and other symbols, but general intelligence is not affected.

Here are a few Famous people who suffered with dyslexia who went on to do remarkable things. Remember, one day your name can be added to this list.

Maggie Aderin-Pocock. Astronomer and space scientist, co-producer of the long-running TV program, 'The Sky at Night' with Chris Lintott...

Orlando Bloom...

Richard Branson...

Tom Cruise...

Leonardo da Vinci...

Walt Disney...

Jim Carrey...

Albert Einstein...

Steven Spielberg...

Whoopi Goldberg...

Understanding Dyslexia: A Condition, not a Disability

Dyslexia, a condition that affects numerous individuals, should never be perceived as a disability. It is crucial to acknowledge that people with dyslexia can lead productive and fulfilling lives, notwithstanding the challenges they may encounter. In the past, dyslexia was stigmatized, unfairly labeling individuals as unintelligent or struggling with reading and writing. However, in our modern world, where language has evolved with the proliferation of abbreviations and acronyms, reading and writing have become more complex for everyone.

Recognizing Dyslexia:
How to Identify the Signs

Identifying dyslexia can be a pivotal step toward obtaining support and overcoming challenges. Common signs include difficulties with reading, spelling, and writing, as well as challenges in understanding sequences and directions. Additionally, individuals with dyslexia may struggle with phonological awareness, impacting their ability to break down and manipulate sounds in words.

Who to Talk to:
Seeking Guidance and Support

If you suspect dyslexia or notice these signs in yourself or someone else, seeking guidance is essential. Start by discussing concerns with teachers, school counselors, or educational professionals. They can provide valuable insights, suggest assessments, and offer recommendations for further evaluation.

Overcoming Stigma:
Changing Perceptions of Dyslexia

It's crucial to dispel the stigma associated with dyslexia and recognize it as a unique way of processing information. Historically, individuals with dyslexia were unfairly judged and labeled, but society's understanding has evolved. By fostering awareness and educating others about the true nature of dyslexia, we contribute to changing perceptions and promoting empathy.

Dyslexia in School:
Advocating for Accommodations

For students with dyslexia, navigating the educational system requires advocacy. Collaborate with teachers and school administrators to implement accommodations tailored to individual needs. This may include alternative learning materials, extended testing times, or specialized instruction. By actively participating in discussions about necessary accommodations, students empower themselves in their academic journey.

Support for Adults:
Embracing Opportunities for Growth

Dyslexia does not limit individuals from pursuing their goals, even in adulthood. Seek assistance from professionals, support groups, or adult education programs that specialize in dyslexia. Embrace opportunities for skill development, whether in reading, writing, or utilizing assistive technologies. By fostering a proactive approach, adults with dyslexia can achieve personal and professional success.

Breaking Barriers:
Overcoming Challenges with Determination

It is crucial to view dyslexia not as a roadblock but as a unique characteristic that can be navigated with determination and support. Cultivate resilience and recognize that challenges do not define one's capabilities. By leveraging strengths and seeking assistance when needed, individuals with dyslexia can pursue their goals, whether in education, career, or personal development.

Conclusion:

Empowering Individuals with Dyslexia

In conclusion, dyslexia should be approached with understanding, empathy, and a commitment to breaking down stigmas. Recognizing the signs, seeking appropriate guidance, and advocating for support in educational and professional settings are essential steps. With determination and a supportive community, individuals with dyslexia can navigate challenges, surpass expectations, and reach their full potential. Dyslexia should never be a hindrance but an opportunity for growth and success.

Chapter 24

Embracing My Unique Journey: Living with Dyslexia

If you are living with dyslexia, it is crucial to embrace your unique wiring as a strength rather than a weakness. Our brains are diverse, and each of us has different talents and abilities. I understand this firsthand, as drafting this book required extra time and effort due to my own challenges with spelling and grammar. Sometimes, I mix up words like "as," "has," or "too," and I often find myself double-checking the correct spelling. Additionally, I may drop or omit certain letters, such as the letter "h." However, these difficulties have not hindered me from drafting this book or achieving success as a businessperson. It is important not to let weaknesses define us or hold us back. Life is what we make of it, and we have the power to choose whether our weaknesses limit us or whether we rise above them and thrive.

I want to emphasize that dyslexia does not negate the multitude of gifts and talents you have. Writing may be a challenge, but it should not overshadow your other abilities. You have the potential to become anything you wish. Do not allow your writing skills to discourage you from pursuing your passions or using your unique talents. Success is within your reach, and it begins with a shift in mindset. Embrace your strengths, focus on what you excel at, and set your sights on achieving your goals. Remember that your dyslexia does not define your worth or decide the course of your life.

In conclusion, dyslexia should never be viewed as a disability. It should be viewed as a unique way of thinking. Despite the misconceptions and challenges associated with dyslexia, many individuals with this condition have gone on to carry out remarkable things. Your dyslexia does not limit your potential or define who you are. You have the power to shape your own destiny and overcome any obstacles that come your way. Believe in yourself, embrace your strengths, and let your unique talents shine. Remember, you can achieve greatness and lead a fulfilling life, regardless of the challenges you face.

"To change perceptions, we must celebrate all that people with dyslexia have achieved so that young people no longer give up before they have even started."

"I'm Not Stupid, Just Unique"

I am not stupid, though letters may dance,

P, B, D, F, H, and eye, in a wild trance.

Thinking differently, a unique view,

Laughed at and called dumb, but that's not true.

Wi did they use too words sounding the same?

As, Has, a puzzle in my mind's game.

Intelligence is not confined to spelling,

Excel in ways that are truly compelling.

Massaging minds, bodies, and souls,

Thinking with hands, not pencils or scrolls.

You return not because I write but feed your soul,

I'm not stupid, because I don't think like you,

Does it make me Dyslexic? Not in my heart.

Allow me to be, let my spirit roam free,

LOL and WYD, a abbreviation language

A language I like because we are all in the same boat,

because no one wants to spell.

Cutting words short,

Not stupidity, just a different mile.

You're not stupid, neither am I,

Spell checks can't measure how high.

BE your kind of beautiful, unique,

In this world where perspectives peak.

Not because of your pen man ship

you will always be unique.

Google and Alexa, friends at your side,

you can make it. Because so did Hi.

Chapter 25

Same-Sex Relationships With Understanding and Respect

Many find themselves grappling with their identities when it comes to relationships. Television and other forms of media often promote same-sex relationships as the norm, but is it truly the only choice?

During my own journey, I contemplated entering a same-sex relationship as a young person. However, I made the personal choice not to pursue it because it did not feel right for me. After experiencing abuse at the hands of men, I did not want to subject myself to any further trauma. I came to realize that the issue lay not in the gender of my partners, but in the individuals, I was choosing to be in relationships with.

It is important to acknowledge that abuse can occur in any relationship, including same-sex relationships. In fact, it can sometimes be even more challenging to discuss abuse within a same-sex partnership. Please understand that being in a same-sex relationship does not guarantee escape from abuse. It is essential to prioritize your safety and well-being in any relationship you enter.

If you choose to explore same-sex relationships, it is crucial to ensure that it is a genuine desire and not something you feel pressured into. When you have experienced pain and betrayal, it is easy to develop biases and make impulsive decisions based on past hurts. Remember that each person is unique, and it is unfair to judge others based on your own experiences. Love and attraction are complex, and nobody has the right to judge your choices.

I once met a young girl who showed tomboyish tendencies and was about to age out of foster care. When we went dress shopping for prom, she expressed a desire for a tuxedo instead. So, we embarked on a journey to find the perfect suit. At one store, she asked for a belt to hold up her pants, which I gladly provided. However, when it came time to buy the pants, she requested female pants instead.

This experience made me realize that she was not necessarily identifying as gay but was using this presentation as a coping mechanism due to the trauma of rape or abuse. Many of us develop coping mechanisms as a response to past traumatic experiences. While these mechanisms help us navigate our daily lives, it is important to equip ourselves with healthy skills to address the underlying issues directly.

In conclusion, navigating relationships and personal identities can be challenging, particularly during adolescence. It is crucial to make choices that align with your true self and prioritize your well-being. Abuse can occur in any relationship, regardless of gender or sexual orientation. Remember that no two people are the same, and it is essential to approach relationships with empathy and understanding. We should focus on building healthy connections based on mutual respect and support, free from judgment and societal expectations.

Chapter 26

COVID-19 and Dating

The landscape of dating has undergone significant changes due to the impact of COVID-19, with online dating becoming increasingly prevalent. However, it is important to approach this new form of dating with caution. While some may believe that dating allows for multiple partners, it is crucial to recognize the risks involved. You never truly know who you are meeting online or whether they engage in multiple sexual relationships. Even in the realm of online dating, care must be taken.

If you are considering entering the dating scene, it is essential to prioritize your health and safety, as sexually transmitted infections (STIs) and AIDS are on the rise. Remember to take the necessary precautions to protect yourself. Effectively using condoms and other forms of contraception can prevent unwanted pregnancies, as well as reduce the risk of STIs that may lead to complications such as pregnancies, sterility, endometriosis, ectopic, and a lifetime of medication.

It is also important to be mindful of your partner's sexual issues, values, and tendencies, even in a same-sex relationship. Open and honest communication is key to keeping a healthy and safe relationship.

Furthermore, if you decide to go on a date, always inform someone you trust of your plans. Leave them with the necessary contact details. Unfortunately, we live in a world where sex trafficking, violence, rape, and date rape are prevalent issues, especially among teenagers. Taking these precautions can help ensure your safety.

In summary, the shift towards online dating in the wake of

COVID-19 needs a heightened awareness of the potential risks involved. Prioritizing your health, taking precautions, and supporting open communication are essential in navigating the dating world. By doing so, you can protect yourself from potential harm and promote healthy and fulfilling relationships.

Research Summaries: Date Rape Among Adolescents - Numerous studies show that lifetime prevalence of date /acquaintance rape ranges from 13%-27% among college-aged women and 20%-68% among adolescents.

Always remember that appearances can be deceiving, especially when it comes to dating. While someone may sound pleasant over the phone or in messages, it is crucial to exercise caution. You never know if you are meeting someone with ill intentions, such as a pedophile. Be mindful and stay vigilant. Additionally, it is important to be aware of the potential presence of drugs or alcohol in the dating scene. Some individuals may initially pretend to be kind and charming but reveal their true colors later. Trust your instincts and prioritize your safety.

Chapter 27

Unveiling the Art of Text Messaging:
A Deeper Dive into the World of Short-form Communication

Numerous studies have shown that texting can trigger significant levels of anxiety. It is also clear that texting can both support and hinder relationships. Whether it serves as a means of staying connected or to avoid challenging conversations, texting has its pros and cons.

When you are feeling down, texting may not be the best form of communication. Misinterpretations can easily occur when the recipient reads your text, leading to feelings of anxiety and abandonment. It is advisable to pick up the phone and call someone when you are feeling low, as it allows for a more direct and personal connection.

Texting can also escalate conflicts, as the way you perceive your own message may differ from how the recipient interprets it. This discrepancy can cause added stress for both parties involved. When conveying important messages, it is preferable to make a call rather than relying on texts.

Lost in Translation:
The Misunderstood Text Message

Coming from England with Jamaican roots, the nuances of language and/or communication can sometimes lead to misunderstandings, especially when interacting with others, like those in America. In a specific incident, a text message I sent to a friend resulted in confusion, leaving us in a prolonged silence. Recognizing the potential for miscommunication, I took the proactive step of calling to clarify my message.

Upon speaking, it became evident that my friend had misconstrued my intentions. Together, we decided that placing more emphasis on phone calls, where tone and nuances are better conveyed, would minimize the chances of misunderstanding in the future. This experience served as a reminder of the importance of being mindful of the content we communicate through text messages, as misinterpretations can strain or even rupture relationships.

Choosing calls over text offers a richer communication experience, allowing the recipient to better perceive the emotions and sincerity behind the words. It's crucial to understand that misinterpretations in text messages can come at a high cost, leading to anger, hurt, and unintended consequences.

By acknowledging the limitations of texting and embracing more direct forms of communication, we can navigate around unnecessary misunderstandings and strengthen our connections. This episode underscores the need for clear and considerate communication, particularly when linguistic and cultural differences are at play. It's a valuable lesson in fostering understanding and building robust relationships.

In conclusion, while texting offers convenience, it is crucial to acknowledge its limitations. When emotions are at stake or significant messages need to be conveyed, a phone call allows for clearer understanding and helps support stronger connections. The prevalence of texting and its associated abbreviations have created a communication barrier between parents and children, contributing to a lack of intimate conversations. Prior to the advent of texting, face-to-face interactions were more common, promoting deeper connections and a better understanding of one another. To bridge this gap, it is important to prioritize direct and personal conversations, as they foster meaningful communication and strengthen relationships. Recognizing the value of intimate conversations, we can overcome the challenges posed by texting and nurture healthier connections with those around us.

Chapter 28

The Impact of Social Media

Social Media refers to the means of interactions among people in which they create, share, and/or exchange information and ideas in virtual communities and networks. The Office of Communications and Marketing manages the main Facebook, Twitter, Instagram, LinkedIn, and YouTube accounts.

Social media has appeared as a significant factor contributing to the increase in suicide, depression, and bullying among children, teenagers, and even adults. Platforms such as Facebook, Instagram, TikTok, and Snapchat have created an illusion that what is portrayed on social media is reality, blurring the lines between fact and fiction. Moreover, the music industry's emphasis on half-naked women, wealth, rap culture, and extravagant lifestyles further perpetuates this distorted sense of reality.

Consequently, young individuals, in their quest for validation and recognition, strive to become the next social media sensation. The pursuit of likes and followers has become an obsession, exerting a detrimental impact on their well-being when their desired level of attention is still unfulfilled. Negative comments on their posts can linger in their minds, undermining their self-esteem and hindering personal growth.

As the desire to please strangers takes precedence, the risk of losing one's identity and developing an addiction to social media platforms becomes all too real. This addiction mirrors the damaging effects of substance abuse highlighting the seriousness of the issue. It is essential to acknowledge that social media itself is not inherently problematic. The key lies in setting up a healthy relationship with these platforms, one that does not dominate our lives or disconnect us from the real world.

To reclaim control over our well-being, we must prioritize genuine experiences and relationships beyond the confines of social media. These needs understanding the limitations of the digital realm and valuing our authentic selves independent of online validation. By finding a balance, we can regain control over our lives, protect our mental health, and foster meaningful connections that extend beyond the virtual space.

Chapter 29

Combating the Surge in Gun Violence

In recent years, there has been a distressing and alarming surge in gun-related violence among children and teenagers, resulting in a significant increase in gun homicides. This surge has brought me face-to-face with numerous parents who have tragically lost their children to gun violence. A common observation is the lack of male figures in many households, leading to a deficit in parental guidance due to work-related demands or stress. Shockingly, firearms have emerged as the leading cause of death for young Americans, permeating our communities and causing irreparable harm.

This rise in violence is not confined to the streets but has infiltrated our schools, where tragic shootings have become an all-too-frequent occurrence, leaving families devastated and communities in mourning. Compounding the issue, many children and teens face the ongoing threat of nonfatal gunshot injuries and various incidents of gun violence.

Despite these alarming trends, some elected officials persist in refusing to take the necessary steps to protect our youth from gun-related crimes. Their obstruction of common-sense gun safety laws, coupled with proposals that could further jeopardize the safety of children and teenagers, is unacceptable and demands a change in approach.

It is imperative to pause and reflect on the profound consequences of gun violence, not only for others but also for ourselves. If we could witness the heart-wrenching scenes of our own family members and loved ones in anguish, grieving over our loss, how would it impact us? While it is easy to empathize with the pain of others, it is crucial to step into someone else's shoes and imagine the devastating impact our actions or inactions could have on our own lives and the lives of those we hold dear.

When we weigh the value of material possessions or transient moments of power against the permanent loss and irreplaceable experiences we risk, the choice becomes clear. Is it worth sacrificing our ability to savor the simple pleasures of life, the love and support of our families, and the opportunities to make a positive impact in the world for temporary gains?

It is high time for a paradigm shift in how we address gun violence, especially concerning the protection of our children and teenagers. Too often, the call for divine intervention follows a tragic incident, whether a child has been murdered or has taken their own life. Yet, why are we not embracing God in our daily lives and helping our children understand that resorting to drugs, getting involved in gangs, and making life-altering decisions are not the answers? Encouraging education as a means to escape a life of crime should be at the forefront of our efforts to guide them toward a brighter future.

To truly address the root causes of gun violence among the youth, we must foster an environment where education, support, and faith are the cornerstones. It is our responsibility to work collectively to protect the well-being of our young people and provide them with the tools they need to navigate life's challenges successfully. Only through a united front and a commitment to change can we hope to break the cycle of violence and ensure a safer, more secure future for the generations to come.

We must prioritize their safety and well-being by advocating for sensible gun laws, supporting comprehensive background checks, and fostering a culture of responsible firearm ownership. By doing so, we can strive to create a future where young lives are no longer cut short, families are spared from immeasurable grief, and our communities are safe from the devastating impact of gun-related crimes.

Ask Yourself These Questions?

That person that bullied you and you decided to kill, is it worth spending the rest of your life in prison?

_____
_____
_____
_____
_____
_____
_____

Is killing someone worth you being raped of your freedom?

_____
_____
_____
_____
_____
_____

Is killing someone worth someone coming back and killing you?

_____
_____
_____
_____
_____
_____
_____

"God Does Exist"

In this room, I lie, surrounded by silence,

No drugs, no crew, just my own defiance.

Once feeling invincible, now consumed by disgrace,

I called out for help but found no saving grace.

Does God love me, I wonder with despair,

Feeling unseen, as if He doesn't even care.

I didn't plan to stray from the path of right,

Yet where was He, when I faced the darkest night?

"My child," I heard a voice, soft and clear,

"I tried to guide you, to help you steer.

The devil tempted you; I saw it in your eyes,

But you turned away, ignoring My cries.

When your mother called, I urged you to stay,

But you slipped out, ignoring My way.

Do you doubt My existence now, My presence nearby?

I wept countless tears, consumed by fear.

I took a bullet meant for you, My love is true,

While another's life was taken, Mine was spared for you.

Your loved ones can visit, write, their hearts not forsaken,

And you can seek knowledge, a future not mistaken.

But imagine, My Child, if you were in the grave,

People mourning, singing songs you didn't crave.

Would you prefer that fate, trapped in eternal pain?

Or embrace My love, which sets you free again?"

In this room, I lie, pondering this plea,

Realizing the depth of love that sets me free.

Though darkness may surround, and questions persist,

God's love endures, a flame that can't be dismissed.

"I am here by your side, in your darkest hour,

My love for you, an everlasting power.

When guilt weighs heavy and loneliness strikes,

Turn to Me, for I am the source of light.

Forgiveness I offer, for every wrong you've done,

My mercy knows no bounds, like the rays of the sun.

My love for you is boundless, beyond your sentence's end,

In every moment, as your Faithful Friend."

So now, I see, that God truly exists,

In my pain and struggles, His love persists.

No matter where life takes me, or what I may face,

God is with me, steadfast in His is endless.

I am here by your side, though you're imprisoned, my love for you cannot be denied. When you doubt your existence, questioning if I'm near, Remember the words of Proverbs 3:5, let faith cast away your fear.

In the mountains of turmoil, where despair takes its toll, give me your worries, for I care for your soul. If guilt weighs heavy, burdening your heart, turn to 1st John 1:9, forgiveness I impart.

When loneliness strikes, leaving you feeling blue, take solace in Hebrews 13:5, for I am always with you.

You do not have to act tough, for I am not part of that crew, For I am your strength and provider, as Philippians 4:19 rings true.

Wisdom and guidance, I will abundantly supply, as 1st Corinthians 1:30 assures, in me, you can rely.

Know that I forgive you, for every wrong you have done, 1 John 1:9 reminds you, my mercy cannot be outrun.

My love for you is boundless, as John 3:16 proclaims, and even beyond your sentence, my presence is still here.

I promise to never leave you, nor forsake you in any way, Hebrews 13:5 reminds you; I am with you every day.

So now, can you see, my child, that I truly exist? In your pain and your struggles, my love persists. No matter the circumstances or where life takes you, I am here, always present, steadfast and true."

Parents, if we want to steer our children away from prison cells, we must prioritize education over trying to be their friend. Gun violence is spiraling out of control, and it's imperative to instill in our children alternative paths, such as entrepreneurship, rather than resorting to illegal activities like drug dealing. We need to do better. When a child succumbs to violence or becomes a perpetrator due to envy or gang conflicts, it's a setup for failure. No postcode or zipcode should dictate whether a child lives or ends up incarcerated because of involvement in drugs. Instead, let's teach them how to navigate the system and avoid the path that leads to wasting their lives behind bars.

Chapter 30

Self-Harming/or Cutting

Definition of Self-Harm by the Mayo Clinic

Overview:

Non-suicidal self-injury, often simply called self-injury, is the act of deliberately harming your own body, such as cutting or burning yourself. It is typically not meant as a suicide attempt. Rather, this type of self-injury is a harmful way to cope with emotional pain, intense anger, and frustration.

While self-injury may bring a momentary sense of calm and a release of tension, it is usually followed by guilt and shame and the return of painful emotions. Although life-threatening injuries are usually not intended, with self-injury comes the possibility of more serious and even fatal self-aggressive actions. Getting the right treatment can help you learn healthier ways to cope.

Some examples of self-harm are skin damage caused by:

- Cutting
- Scratching
- Self-Battery
- Knocking
- Pinching
- Biting
- Burning
- Wearing Long Sleeves

The prevalence of self-harm among children aged 14 to 17 is a concerning issue that demands attention. It is important for parents to recognize that their child may not openly discuss this behavior, making it even more crucial to be vigilant and supportive. Self-harm often serves as a misguided coping mechanism, a silent plea for help in the face of overwhelming emotions.

Children or adults who engage in self-harm may not fully understand the reasons behind their actions. They might be grappling with familial challenges, feeling isolated or left out, or silently carrying burdens such as academic stress, bullying, or the relentless pressures of social media.

As parents, it is imperative to foster an open and non-judgmental environment that encourages communication. Initiate conversations with your child about their well-being, emotions, and any difficulties they may be facing. Show empathy and understanding, assuring them that you are there to support and listen without criticism or judgment.

It is also crucial to educate yourself about self-harm, its underlying causes, and available resources. Professional help, such as therapy or counseling, can play a pivotal role in aiding your child in finding healthier coping mechanisms and addressing the root causes of their distress.

Be vigilant for signs of self-harm, such as unexplained injuries, frequent wearing of concealing clothing, or a sudden avoidance of situations that may expose their self-inflicted wounds. However, keep in mind that self-harm can be a deeply personal and secretive act, so relying solely on visible signs may not supply a complete picture of your child's struggles.

Remember that your child's well-being is of utmost importance. Approach the situation with empathy, patience, and unconditional love. Encourage open dialogue, seek professional help when needed, and work together to find healthier ways to navigate the challenges your child may be facing.

Bearing My Scars:
A Personal Reflection on Self-Harm

Reflecting on my childhood and adulthood, I feel compelled to share my personal self-harm journey. During that time, I was unaware that my actions formed self-harm. I did not want to end my life; rather, I sought physical pain to match the emotional turmoil I was experiencing. The weight of being bullied and treated as insignificant, particularly during my bus rides, drove me to try slashing my wrists with a razor blade. However, the sight of blood overwhelmed me, and my attempts to find solace through pills proved unsuccessful due to their unpleasant side effects.

Back then, self-harm was misunderstood and unrecognized. It was a taboo subject, rarely spoken about openly. Considering this, I want to emphasize to parents the importance of remaining vigilant and perceptive when it comes to changes in their child's behavior. Even if you are grappling with your own challenges, such as a troubled marriage, work-related stress, or financial problems, it is still essential to prioritize your child's well-being. They, too, are enduring their own pain.

Recognizing and addressing self-harm needs creating an open dialogue within families. It requires supplying a safe and non-judgmental space for children to express their emotions. If self-harm is suspected or discovered, seeking professional help promptly is crucial. Mental health professionals can guide the child and the family towards healthier coping mechanisms and understanding the underlying causes.

Let us work together to cultivate a society that acknowledges and understands self-harm, and where support is readily available for those who need it. By sharing our stories, we can promote awareness, empathy, and the hope of a brighter future.

I want you to know that you are not alone in your struggles. There are many others who understand and empathize with what you are going through. The feelings of being lost, unloved, and unheard can be overwhelming, but it is important to remember that self-harm is not the solution. You are unique, valuable, and deserving of love and care.

Reach out to someone you trust, whether it is a supportive indivual, a friend, or a helpline. Sharing your feelings and experiences can help lighten the burden you carry. You do not have to face these challenges alone.

Instead of turning to self-harm, explore healthier ways to cope with stress and difficult emotions:

Surround yourself with friends who uplift and support you. Spending time with positive influences can bring joy and supply a sense of belonging.

Prioritize getting enough sleep. Restorative rest can improve your overall well-being and help you face challenges with more clarity and resilience.

Discover activities or hobbies that bring you fulfillment and allow you to express yourself. Engaging in creative outlets, sports, or other interests can supply a healthy outlet for emotions and help you develop a sense of accomplishment.

Challenge negative thoughts and replace them with positive affirmations. You can find empowering and uplifting resources on platforms like YouTube and social media that offer encouragement and guidance.

Remember, there is hope for a brighter future, and there are people who genuinely care about your well-being. By reaching out and seeking support, you can find the strength and resilience within yourself to navigate through these grim times. You deserve happiness, love, and support. You are not alone, and there are brighter days ahead.

Self-Evaluation

Find Your Negative Self-Evaluations. To help you do that, first ask yourself:

What is the situation I am in?

_____

_____

_____

_____

_____

What am I saying to myself?

_____

_____

_____

_____

How am I evaluating myself?

_____

_____

_____

_____

_____

How am I putting myself down?

_____

_____

_____

_____

_____

How am I criticizing myself?

_____

_____

_____

_____

_____

Journal

Ask Yourself These Important Questions:

- Does anyone threaten to hurt you or other people you care about?

- Do they hit, kick, punch, push, choke or use physical force against you?

- Do they criticize or blame you for everything that goes wrong?

- Do they humiliate you in front of other people?

- Do they control your access to money?

- Do they control the decision-making in your relationship?

- Do they control your time and actions'?

- Do they put you down, call you names, and make you feel like you are weird?

- Do they destroy your property or abuse your pets?

- Do they threaten to hurt you or commit suicide if you leave?

- Do they force or coerce you to have sex when you do not want to?

Journal

Chapter 31

Raising Awareness on Mental Illness

Educating both adults and teens about mental illness and suicide is vital. By arming ourselves with knowledge, we're encouraged to openly discuss these issues and seek help when needed. Many individuals struggle to confide in others due to busy schedules or personal emotional challenges, leading to increased suffering, depression, and suicidal thoughts, especially among adolescents.

To protect and empower our loved ones, it's crucial to train individuals to identify vulnerable students. Teachers can benefit from self-awareness training to better understand their students' struggles. Moreover, professionals should conduct training sessions to equip teachers with the skills to effectively support vulnerable students. Implementing educational initiatives like informative posters can also help spread awareness and reduce the stigma surrounding mental health.

Additionally, there should be a safe and confidential reporting system for teenagers to report concerns about their peers without facing repercussions. This system ensures that potential warning signs are addressed promptly.

Teachers should regularly report significant changes in students' behavior to address issues like suicide and abuse. Every school should have a well-defined strategy to handle these issues. However, addressing suicide requires a comprehensive approach involving multiple stakeholders.

When a child aged 10 or older displays signs of distress, such as physical pain or mental anguish, it should prompt a clinical assessment to identify potential suicidal tendencies. Education and training by medical professionals are essential to recognize and respond to these issues effectively. Having emergency staff available in schools is crucial for handling crisis situations, with ongoing support and aftercare measures prioritized for at-risk students.

In conclusion, addressing suicide requires a multifaceted approach, including awareness programs, teacher training, reporting mechanisms, clinical assessments, medical expertise, and comprehensive support systems. By implementing these strategies, we can create a safer and more supportive environment for our youth, ultimately saving lives and promoting mental well-being.

Why Intervention is Important:

Parenting is both rewarding and challenging, requiring constant attention to our children's needs. However, amidst the busyness of life, it's easy to overlook signs of distress in our children. Our own desires and obligations can often take precedence, inadvertently causing us to miss subtle signals indicating our children may be struggling.

Reflecting on my experience as a teenage parent, I recall the overwhelming sense of responsibility coupled with the absence of a clear guidebook. Navigating parenthood without a roadmap left me questioning if I was adequately meeting my child's needs.

It's crucial to recognize these blind spots in our lives. The demands of work, personal aspirations, and social engagements can overshadow our children's needs, making it crucial to actively listen and create a safe space for them to express themselves.

Being attuned to our children's well-being requires proactive effort. By setting aside dedicated time for meaningful interactions and actively listening to their concerns, we foster trust and openness.

In parenting, acknowledging our vulnerabilities is essential. While none of us have a foolproof manual, we can educate ourselves, seek guidance, and participate in supportive communities.

As we navigate parenthood, it's vital to remain resilient and adaptable, adjusting our strategies to meet our children's evolving needs.

In conclusion, acknowledging our blind spots prompts us to be intentional in parenting, fostering open communication and creating a nurturing environment where our children feel understood and supported.

Chapter 32

Understanding and Overcoming Peer Pressure

Peer pressure is an influence one or more people have on a person. This usually happens between friends and acquaintances.

Signs of Peer Pressure:

- Increased irritability.

- Reckless behavior that seems out of character.

- Substance Abuse.

- Sudden change in attitude, behavior, or beliefs.

- Teens develop a desire to fit in with their friends /acquaintances and be accepted by them.

- Often related to age-appropriate behavior

What are The Main Causes of Peer Pressure?

Peer Pressure Example

When starting at a new school or job, we are eager to fit in and make friends. However, you may find yourself pressured into joining a certain group and engaging in activities that go against your true character. You feel compelled to smoke, drink, do drugs, or even shoplift, simply because you fear being ridiculed by others. In these moments, it is important to remember that you always have a choice. You can choose to walk away from these negative influences and seek out new friends and acquaintances who align with your values

It is crucial to understand that giving in to such pressures carries consequences, and even if you comply, you may still not find the acceptance you are looking for. Never allow anyone to push you out of your comfort zone and change the essence of who you truly are and who you are meant to be. Stay true to yourself, your values, and your principles, even if it means standing apart from the crowd. Your individuality and authenticity are far more valuable than any temporary acceptance gained through compromising your integrity.

Remember that devoted friends will appreciate you for who you genuinely are and will respect your boundaries. Surround yourself with people who uplift and support you, allowing you to grow and flourish while staying true to yourself. Making choices that align with your values will lead you down a path of self-discovery, personal growth, and meaningful connections.

So, if you ever find yourself facing these pressures, take a moment to reflect on your true worth and the kind of person you aspire to be. Trust yourself and have the courage to walk away from situations that compromise your integrity. Embrace your uniqueness and seek friendships based on mutual respect and shared values. By staying true to yourself, you will attract genuine connections and build a fulfilling and authentic life.

How to Deal with Peer Pressure

- Practice saying "NO."
- Get away from the "Peer Pressure Zone."

- Avoid stressful situations in the first place.
- Always use the buddy system.
- Ask 101 questions.
- Say "No" like you mean it.
- Back up a No with a positive statement Be repetitive.

Example:

As Alexis walked home from one day, she bumped into her best friend, Denise, who mentioned going to her aunt's house. Curiously, Denise asked Alexis if she had ever tried smoking weed before. Firmly, Alexis responded, "No way! I have no interest in that." Denise persisted, saying, "Oh, come on! I took it from my brother's room so we can get high. What are you afraid of?" Confused by her friend's insistence, Alexis stood her ground, realizing that compromising her values was not worth it. Denise laughed and walked away, saying, "You'd be a lot cooler if you did!"

In that moment, Alexis recognized the importance of staying true to herself and making choices aligned with her own beliefs. She understood that succumbing to peer pressure would only lead her away from her comfort zone and the person she wanted to be. Although Denise's words lingered in her mind, Alexis remained confident in her decision to resist the temptation.

Alexis knew that her worth was not defined by conforming to societal expectations or engaging in activities that did not align with her values. She valued her individuality and the principles that guided her actions. Even if it meant potentially facing ridicule or being labeled as "uncool," she embraced the strength to stay true to herself.

As the days went by, Alexis found solace in the friendships that celebrated her authenticity and respected her choices. She surrounded herself with people who uplifted and supported her, appreciating her for who she genuinely was. Through this experience, Alexis learned that faithful friends accept and embrace each other's differences without pressuring or undermining their individuality.

From that day forward, Alexis carried the lesson with her, reminding herself to trust her instincts and stand firm in her values, no matter the circumstances. She understood that genuine friendships and personal growth could only be nurtured by staying true to herself and never compromising her integrity.

So, despite the tempting words and fleeting laughter of Denise, Alexis walked away with a newfound sense of self-assurance. She knew that her choices mattered, and she had the power to shape her own path. With each step, she embraced her uniqueness and confidently moved forward, Un swayed by the opinions and actions of others.

Discussion: If someone I knew tried to influence me to engage in activities that went against my values, I would firmly assert my boundaries and explain why I chose not to take part.

_____

_____

_____

_____

_____

_____

_____

_____

_____

_____

_____

_____

_____

_____

_____

_____

_____

Chapter 33

Embracing Beauty Beyond Skin

Reflecting on my childhood, memories of feelings of inadequacy and unworthiness surface prominently. In a family where physical appearances varied, I often found myself the target of hurtful comments due to my dark skin, being tall and skinny, prominent nose, and full lips, inherited from my mother. The comparisons to Olive Oil from Popeye stung, and I endured being called terrible names like "Blackie" and "Monkey." These experiences led to tears, sleepless nights, and a skewed understanding of beauty.

Growing up, I internalized the belief that my looks would hinder my chances of finding love, a notion debunked later in life when I realized Olive Oil had two suitors vying for her affection. This realization prompted me to reconsider the conventional standards of beauty and recognize that true beauty extends far beyond physical appearances. Understanding that we are all made in the image of God became a crucial part of reclaiming my self-worth.

Beauty, I discovered, is a multifaceted concept. It transcends the superficial and delves into realms of kindness, compassion, strength, and the potential to make a positive impact on others. This broader perspective enabled me to appreciate the unique qualities that make me who I am and to redefine my understanding of beauty.

It's essential to remember that your worth is not contingent upon how well you align with societal beauty norms. True beauty emanates from within, fueled by your character, actions, and the ability to contribute positively to the world. Embracing this truth allows you to reclaim your self-worth and acknowledge that you deserve love, respect, and happiness, irrespective of societal expectations.

In the journey to self-love, it's crucial to recognize that the opinions of others about your physical appearance do not define your value. You possess the power to shape your narrative and define your self-worth. Don't allow anyone to project their insecurities onto you; often, those who attempt to bring others down are fueled by jealousy and recognize something admirable within you. Hold your head high, embrace your uniqueness, and let your inner beauty shine.

Self-worth is intricately tied to understanding that God loves you just as you are. Your worth is not determined by external judgments but by the unconditional love and acceptance you receive from a higher power. Embrace the truth that you are fearfully and wonderfully made, deserving of all the love and goodness life has to offer.

In conclusion, my journey from insecurity to self-love involved a redefinition of beauty, an appreciation for my uniqueness, and the acknowledgment that true beauty is not confined to physical attributes. Embrace your authenticity, hold onto your self-worth, and allow the radiance of your inner beauty to illuminate your path.

UGLY ME

Something is wrong with me,

To make others hurt me that way

I didn't hit them or say mean things,

So I'm at a loss as to what to think or say.

What do I say about such actions?

How do I begin to explain?

It happened as a child, in my teens,

and beyond, and I still can't make it plain.

That's how I've always seen myself

– Plain, Homely, and Scarred.

My siblings were all so smart, lovely, and cute, unlike me.

Dumb, Ugly, and Marred.

So, I took the pain and hid all the tears, and told No One,

Because it was probably all my fault.

Losing my virginity to a violent rape,

Too young to know that it was assault.

Not just men, but women too,

But whoever heard of that?

So, I figured that if I could destroy what they wanted.

I'd be free of another attack.

Now I know that it wasn't my body at all,

But my spirit that drew them all near,

But they were not worthy of such a prize,

So they tried to control it with fear.

And for a long time, it worked.

I hid. I called myself ugly, too.

And no matter the compliment or encouraging word,

My fear and pain would let nothing get through.

But THE FATHER kept pushing me out in front,

As I kept trying to hide.

HE gave me a gift of great size,

That keeps me by HIS PRECIOUS SIDE.

I now understand that it was all in HIS PLAN,

Though tough, it needed to be.

For this gift is not for my enjoyment alone,

But to help others to know HIS LOVE,

And heal and find their own unique beauty.

By Elle Crawford-Thomas

"Who I am is What I am"

What I am is who I am.

I'm a proud Black woman.

They say I am an African.

My color is dark.

My eyes are white.

Just like the stars that shine at night.

My lips are thick.

They say they are the best kissing lips.

My hair is like wool.

Just like the duvet the keeps you warm on a cold winter night.

My shoulders are broad.

They need to be cause of the remarks that sometime hurts me.

Who I am is what I am.

What I am is who I am.

I'm the leaves that blow with nowhere to go.

I'm the bird that sings when I'm filled with joy.

I'm the monkey that chatters when I need a natter.

I'm the sun that shines when I'm alive.

I am the rain that falls when things matter.

I'm the playful child with that cheeky grin.

I'm your friend, you see, I'm everything.

Who I am is what I am.

What I am is who I am.

I'm as free as the wind spreading everything within.

You might not like me for who I am.

I can be miserable at times.

I talk from my heart.

God promised me he will be by my side.

Even in pain, I hold my head high.

I wear my crown.

Cause I'm a proud Black woman.

I am a British, Jamaican, and now an American

It's not the color of my skin that makes me,

Who I am or what I am.

What I am, Is who I am.

I'm Valerie!

I'm Valerie.

Questions you can ask yourself?

What are your most recurring thoughts?

_____

_____

_____

_____

How do you feel right now, and why?

_____

_____

_____

_____

What are some things you do not like about yourself?

_____

_____

_____

_____

Why do you not like these things?

_____

_____

_____

_____

What are things that make you happy and feeling good?

_____

_____

_____

_____

What are your happiest memories, and why?

Can you pick your favorite color and draw how you feel

Describe your favorite person.

_____

_____

_____

_____

What would you tell yourself right now?

_____

_____

_____

_____

What are 3 things you like about yourself?

_____

_____

_____

_____

Chapter 34

Gaslighting and Narcissism

"Gaslighting and Narcissism: Understanding the Difference and Recognizing the Signs of Victimization"

Gaslighting and narcissism are terms often used interchangeably, yet they represent distinct psychological phenomena with different manifestations and impacts on individuals. Understanding these differences is crucial for identifying and addressing the signs of victimization.

Gaslighting is a form of psychological manipulation aimed at making the victim doubt their own perceptions, memories, and sanity. It involves the gradual erosion of the victim's self-confidence and trust in their own judgment, leaving them vulnerable to the gaslighter's control. Gaslighting tactics typically include denying the victim's reality, trivializing their feelings and experiences, and shifting blame onto them for the gaslighter's actions.

On the other hand, narcissism refers to a personality trait characterized by grandiosity, a sense of entitlement, a lack of empathy, and a constant need for admiration and validation. Narcissists often manipulate and exploit others to fulfill their own needs, viewing them as mere extensions of themselves rather than autonomous individuals. While not all narcissists engage in gaslighting, the two behaviors frequently coexist, particularly in abusive relationships.

Recognizing the signs of gaslighting and narcissism can help individuals identify if they are victims of such manipulation. Some common indicators of gaslighting include:

1. Doubting one's own perceptions and memories.

2. Feeling confused, anxious, or insecure.

3. Having difficulty making decisions or trusting oneself.

4. Apologizing excessively, even when not at fault.

5. Isolating oneself from friends and family due to the gaslighter's influence.

6. Experiencing mood swings or changes in behavior without apparent cause.

7. Feeling constantly on edge or walking on eggshells around the gaslighter.

In contrast, signs of narcissistic victimization may include:

1. Feeling used or exploited by the narcissist for their own gain.

2. Experiencing emotional manipulation, such as guilt-tripping or love bombing.

3. Feeling invalidated or dismissed when expressing one's thoughts or feelings.

4. Experiencing emotional or psychological abuse, such as verbal attacks or silent treatment.

5. Feeling controlled or stifled in the relationship, with little room for autonomy or independence.

6. Experiencing a sense of emptiness or worthlessness as a result of the narcissist's behavior.

7. Having difficulty establishing boundaries or asserting oneself in the relationship.

It's important to note that being a victim of gaslighting or narcissism is not a reflection of one's character or worth. These behaviors stem from the insecurities and maladaptive coping mechanisms of the gaslighter or narcissist, rather than any inherent flaw in the victim.

If you suspect that you are a victim of gaslighting or narcissism, it's essential to seek support from trusted friends, family members, or mental health professionals. Building a support network and developing self-awareness can help you regain confidence in your own perceptions and break free from the cycle of manipulation and abuse. Additionally, setting boundaries and seeking therapy can empower you to assert yourself and prioritize your emotional well-being in relationships. Remember, you deserve to be treated with respect, empathy, and kindness, and no one has the right to undermine your sense of self-worth.

MY STORY
Escaping Gaslighting and Narcissistic Abuse

My daughter's father used to manipulate me into believing I had done things I knew I hadn't. Despite his gaslighting attempts, I found refuge in meditation, which helped me trace my steps throughout the day and reaffirm my innocence. Back then, we lacked the vocabulary to understand his tactics, leading to arguments and even physical abuse, all while he portrayed a different persona to the outside world.

When I moved to the USA with my ex-husband, he projected an image of success, despite his actual occupation as a substitute teacher.

Behind closed doors, he would provoke me into reactions and then twist the situation to shift blame onto me. Many of us endure such relationships out of fear of violence, believing no one will believe our truth.

It wasn't until my family visited from England in 2015 and introduced me to the concepts of narcissism and gaslighting that I began to grasp the gravity of my situation. This awakening prompted me to establish the Purple Light Touch Foundation, exclusively for women and girls, to safeguard our safe space from contamination. Despite his demeaning words and financial manipulation, I found the strength to speak up and reclaim my autonomy.

If you're enduring similar abuse, know that you're not alone. Your voice matters, and there are people who will listen. I've walked this path, and I refuse to let a narcissist manipulate or gaslight another woman. You have a voice—don't hesitate to use it!

Chapter 35

Teenage Pregnancy

Teenage pregnancy is pregnancy in females under the age of 18, having not reached the legal age of adulthood, which can vary from place to place. The main cause of teen pregnancy is a lack of awareness by the teen that they can become pregnant when ovulation begins, which can be before her first menstrual period, though that is not common.

Many parents need to take off the blinders and realize that their children are sexually aware and could be sexually active. Many parents will try to shield their children from discussions related to sex and from being sexually active because of their own past as it relates to sex.

What Are the Causes of Teenage Pregnancy?

- Peer Pressure. During adolescence, teenagers often feel pressure to make friends and fit in with their peers.
- Absent Parents.
- Glamorization of Pregnancy.
- Lack of Knowledge.
- Sexual Abuse or Rape.
- Teenage Drinking.

Teen Pregnancy: Navigating Influences and Challenges

Adolescence, marked by the transitional journey from childhood to adulthood, is a phase where teenagers grapple with various pressures, and one prevalent challenge is teen pregnancy. Several factors contribute to the complex landscape of teenage pregnancy, ranging from peer pressure to a lack of parental guidance and societal influences.

Peer pressure is a powerful force during adolescence, as teenagers strive to build friendships and find acceptance within their peer groups. The desire to fit in can lead to risky behaviors, including engaging in unprotected sexual activities, which may contribute to unintended pregnancies.

The absence of parental guidance can leave teenagers without a stable support system to navigate the challenges of adolescence. Without proper guidance, teenagers may be more susceptible to making uninformed decisions regarding their sexual health, increasing the risk of unintended pregnancies.

The glamorization of pregnancy in media and popular culture can inadvertently influence many teenagers' perceptions. Misrepresentation of the challenges and responsibilities associated with parenthood may downplay the gravity of the situation, potentially contributing to a casual attitude towards sexual activities.

Lack of knowledge about sexual health and contraceptives is a significant factor in teen pregnancies. Inadequate sexual education or a lack of open conversations about reproductive health can leave teenagers uninformed about the risks and preventive measures, increasing the likelihood of unintended pregnancies.

Tragically, some teenagers face the harrowing reality of sexual abuse or rape, which can result in unwanted pregnancies. These traumatic experiences not only impact their emotional well-being but also pose unique challenges when it comes to addressing the pregnancy and its aftermath.

Teenage drinking is another contributing factor to the complex issue of teen pregnancy. Impaired judgment under the influence of alcohol may lead to risky behaviors, including unprotected sex, thereby elevating the risk of unintended pregnancies.

Addressing teen pregnancy requires a multifaceted approach that involves comprehensive sexual education, open communication between parents and teenagers, and fostering a supportive community. Providing accurate information about sexual health, contraception, and the consequences of early parenthood can empower teenagers to make informed choices.

Creating an environment where teenagers feel comfortable discussing their concerns and questions is crucial. Open communication channels with parents, educators, and peers can help demystify misconceptions and equip teenagers with the knowledge and resilience needed to navigate the challenges associated with adolescence and sexual health.

In essence, addressing teen pregnancy involves recognizing the multifactorial influences at play and implementing comprehensive strategies to empower teenagers with the tools and information they need to make responsible choices about their sexual health.

Chapter 36

Teenage Pregnancy: My Personal Journey

During my teenage years, at the tender age of 15, my life took an unexpected turn when I found myself facing an unplanned pregnancy. The circumstances surrounding my relationship were far from ideal, as I stayed with my partner out of a sense of obligation and necessity. His claims of being in need due to a stabbing incident played on my sympathies, keeping me entangled in a loveless relationship. Insecurities stemming from years of bullying further contributed to my decision, as I believed the lies that no one else would ever show interest in me.

This unforeseen pregnancy shattered the carefully crafted plans I had envisioned for my future. I had dreams of exploring the world and becoming a childcare provider, but now fear consumed me as I grappled with the overwhelming uncertainty of my situation. Carrying the weight of this secret alone took its toll on me, affecting my physical and emotional well-being. I found myself unable to eat and plagued by daily sickness, but amidst a large family, my struggles went unnoticed.

I soldiered on, concealing my pregnancy even as I sat through state tests, with no one suspecting the truth I carried within. In England, the choice to officially leave school at the age of 15 was available, granted one's birthday did not fall in September. Mine fell in June, leaving me with only a few months before I could legally leave school, all while bearing the weight of my hidden secret.

My mother's reaction added another layer of complexity to an already challenging situation. She was angry, feeling that I had brought shame to the family. However, amidst the turmoil, my father exhibited compassion and support, making the remaining months of my pregnancy more bearable. It was a stark contrast in reactions within my own family.

The hospital suggested the option of giving up my daughter for adoption, but my determination to keep and raise my child prevailed. Being a teenage mom while still living at home presented numerous challenges—sleepless nights, the responsibility of another life, and the absence of the typical experiences of adolescence.

To those who may find themselves experiencing similar emotions and uncertainties, please know that you are not alone. It is crucial to reach out and seek support from trusted individuals who can supply guidance and understanding during this challenging time. Remember that circumstances may change, and there is always hope for the future, even when it seems uncertain. Life has a way of surprising us, and with the right support and determination, you can find your way through unexpected turns and create a fulfilling path for yourself.

Embracing the strength within you and remembering that your journey is unique is key. Despite the obstacles you may face, never lose sight of your dreams and aspirations. Your worth and potential extend far beyond the circumstances you find yourself in today. Seek out the resources available to you, lean on the support of loved ones, and take small steps toward creating a future that aligns with your true desires. You have the power to overcome challenges and shape your own destiny.

Raising a child is a lifelong commitment that requires immense dedication. It is not a temporary responsibility that can be easily cast aside.

If the baby's father is absent or unwilling to be involved, unless you have a dedicated support system, caring for the child can become burdensome and challenging. I was fortunate to have a loving network of family and friends who stood by me during that tough time, but I know that many of you may not be as fortunate.

Before engaging in sexual activity or risking pregnancy, it is crucial to take precautions. If a partner refuses to use protection like condoms, it is a clear sign that they may not be the right person for you. Love can sometimes blind us, giving us a false sense of security. It is essential to consider who will be left to shoulder the responsibility of caring for a child – and it will be you.

I share my story to emphasize the importance of making informed choices and protecting ourselves before entering intimate relationships. Your future and well-being deserve careful consideration. Remember that you are in control of your own destiny and have the power to shape your life. Surround yourself with people who respect and support you, and never settle for less than what you deserve.

Chapter 37

Single, Doesn't Mean I'm Alone

Today, there is a misconception that being single is equivalent to committing a crime. The pressure to have a boyfriend or girlfriend can make individuals feel as though something is inherently wrong with them. However, the truth is that the single phase of life is a valuable opportunity for self-discovery and personal growth. During this time, you can consider whether your desires are non-negotiable.

Being single is not a crime; being in the wrong relationship is. It is crucial not to succumb to societal expectations and rush into relationships just because someone claims to love you. Love should never be a justification for mistreatment. You may find yourself entangled with someone who is involved with multiple partners, resulting in heartbreak and pain.

It is normal to go through several partners before finding the right one. Embrace your single status and take the time to reflect on the qualities you look for in a partner. Observe how potential partners interact with their family, their sense of style, their work ethic, and how they treat you. Prioritize this evaluation process before entering a meaningful relationship, as it can help you avoid becoming a teenage parent or getting involved in an abusive relationship.

Self-Discovery and Embracing the Single Life

After the tumultuous chapter with my ex-husband, I made a

deliberate choice to embark on a journey of self-discovery and embrace the single life. It was a conscious decision, a commitment to focus on myself, my needs, and my well-being. Little did I know, this period of singleness would be one of the most transformative phases of my life.

Leaving a marriage is no small feat, and the decision to be single afterward was both empowering and liberating. It allowed me the space to understand myself on a profound level, to establish firm boundaries, and to gain clarity on what I truly desired in a relationship. This period of solitude became a canvas for me to paint my own portrait of happiness.

Crucially, being single does not equate to loneliness. Instead, it is an invaluable opportunity for self-exploration and growth. It's a time to rediscover your passions, redefine your standards, and revel in the freedom of choice. By deliberately choosing to be single, I laid the groundwork for a future relationship that would be built on a foundation of self-love and personal fulfillment.

In the process of self-discovery, I learned the importance of nurturing my relationship with myself. It's about taking the time to truly know who you are, to appreciate your strengths and acknowledge your areas for growth. This introspective period allowed me to define my values, aspirations, and non-negotiables in life and love.

Love, in its purest form, began with self-love. I engaged in self-care practices, meditated to find peace within, and took moments to reflect on my journey. Looking in the mirror became a symbolic act of self-acceptance, appreciating the person I saw looking back at me. It was an opportunity to forge a deep connection with myself, fostering a love that became the cornerstone of my newfound strength.

Spending quality time with myself became a cherished ritual. I embraced solitary activities that brought me joy, whether it was reading a book, taking long walks, or indulging in creative pursuits. These moments of solitude allowed me to savor my own company and reinforced the idea that being alone is not synonymous with loneliness.

I took the pen into my own hands and began to write my affirmations. Affirmations that spoke of self-worth, resilience, and the power of choice. This practice became a daily reminder of my journey, a narrative that I was actively shaping. I was crafting a new story that was rooted in self-love and defined by the strength to choose myself over and over again.

Through this process, I fell in love with myself. It wasn't a narcissistic love, but a genuine appreciation for the person I had become. I knew what I wanted, what I deserved, and what I would not accept in any future relationship. This self-awareness became my guiding compass, steering me away from settling for anything less than I deserved.

So, to anyone feeling the weight of singleness, I say this: embrace it as an opportunity for self-renewal. Take the time to love yourself, to know yourself, and to become the architect of your own happiness. Being single is not a void to be filled; it is a canvas waiting for you to paint the masterpiece of your own love story.

Chapter 38

A Guide to Grief Support and Emotional Recovery

Grief support plays a crucial role in helping individuals rebuild their lives and regain focus after experiencing loss, tragedy, or misfortune. The intense sorrow associated with grief can be overwhelming, and that's when grief counseling becomes necessary.

Grief counseling aims to aid individuals who are deeply affected by their grief, to the point where their usual coping mechanisms are no longer effective. It supplies a safe and supportive space for individuals to express their emotions and thoughts about their loss. This can include feelings of sadness, anxiety, anger, loneliness, guilt, relief, confusion, and numbness. Through counseling, individuals can explore these emotions and find healthy ways to navigate the challenges that arise from loss, as well as cope with the changes it brings to their lives. Additionally, common symptoms such as disorganization, fatigue, difficulty concentrating, sleep disturbances, vivid dreams, and changes in appetite can be addressed in counseling sessions.

Grief counseling also supports individuals in resolving their natural reactions to loss, particularly when their grief has overwhelmed their ability to cope. Thankfully, there are many online resources available that supply comprehensive information on grief and loss counseling. One valuable example is The Grief Counseling Resource Guide offered by The New York State Office of Mental Health.

Anticipatory grief is another circumstance where grief counseling can be beneficial. This type of grief occurs when individuals experience frequent intrusive thoughts and worries about the imminent or expected death of a loved one, or when a loved one has been diagnosed with a terminal illness. Anticipatory grief presents unique challenges, often impairing a person's ability to remain present while simultaneously grappling with the impending loss. Counseling can help individuals navigate the complexities of anticipatory grief, including the process of holding on, letting go, and drawing closer to the dying individual. It can also help individuals examine the parts of themselves that they may feel they will lose in the process.

In conclusion, grief counseling supplies essential support and guidance to individuals navigating the complexities of grief. By addressing emotions, easing coping strategies, and fostering resolution, grief counseling plays a pivotal role in helping individuals rebuild their lives, find healing, and create a new sense of normalcy after experiencing profound loss.

Grieving Alone

Grieving is a natural and integral part of our human experience, and it is important to remember that there is no shame in allowing ourselves to grieve. During our childhood, some of us may have been taught to hide our emotions or suppress our tears, leading us to believe that grieving is something to be ashamed of. However, it is crucial to understand that grieving alone is different from openly acknowledging and processing our grief.

If you find yourself in a challenging situation where you instinctively respond with "I'm alright" when you are not, it is an opportunity to reach out for help and support. Trusted friends, family members, or professionals are there to supply guidance and help during challenging times. There is no prescribed time limit for grief, and it can surface at any point in our lives, even years after a loss. Grief can take different forms, extending beyond the loss of a person through death and encompassing other significant life traumas.

It is important to recognize that grief involves a range of emotions, including sadness, confusion, and unanswered questions. Seeking support and sharing your grief with others is not a sign of weakness but rather an act of bravery and self-care. By surrounding yourself with a supportive network, you can find solace, understanding, and guidance throughout the grieving process.

Everyone's journey through grief is unique, and it is crucial to grant yourself permission to grieve in your own time and way. Embracing your grief and acknowledging its presence opens the door to healing and eventual acceptance. By treating yourself with compassion and prioritizing self-care, you can navigate the complexities of loss and find the strength to move forward on your path of healing.

Chapter 39

Understanding Grief and Finding Strength

In the past, stories of loss shared by friends seemed distant to me, as my immediate family members were still alive. I couldn't fully grasp the depth of their emotions, and even when I faced a miscarriage, expressing my own feelings became a struggle. It wasn't until the loss of my grandson that the true nature of pain became clear. I found myself pleading with God to spare me and take me instead.

The turning point arrived with the loss of my father. Everything changed, and the impact of loss became tangible. I finally understood the longing to hear "daddy" or the absence of cherished visits. The loss had a profound effect, and I realized that the pain it brings is unlike any other.

Experiencing loss firsthand opened my eyes to the profound hurt it entails. Grief is a force that shapes our understanding of empathy and compassion. These experiences highlighted the importance of acknowledging and confirming the pain of others and offering support and understanding during their moments of loss.

In 2017, the cumulative weight of grief hit me not just for my father, who passed away in 2003, but also for my grandson in 2000 and nephew in 2017, a day before my birthday. The tears flowed, bringing out body trauma in my right hip from overwhelming emotions. Additionally, discovering my husband's infidelity added unwanted stress to my body. Through the journey of grief, I've discovered that time doesn't possess a magical ability to heal wounds. Instead, healing is a nuanced process involving reflection, refocusing, and learning to cope with triggers. The passage of time alone doesn't erase the pain; it's the intentional effort to confront and navigate the emotions that foster true healing.

Grief is not a linear experience; it's an ongoing journey that requires patience and self-compassion. Unexpected moments may act as triggers, resurfacing buried emotions and reminding us of the profound impact of loss. In those moments, I've learned to embrace the waves of grief, allowing myself the space to feel and process the emotions that arise. Through this process, I've found strength in acknowledging the complexity of grief and the importance of self-care during the ongoing healing journey.

Journal

Chapter 40

Anxious Attachment Style

Anxious attachment is **one of the types of insecure attachment styles**. Children with anxious attachment express distress when their caregiver leaves and are difficult to soothe when they return. They behave as if they are not certain that they can rely upon the caregiver and show some resentment at being abandoned.

Signs of Anxious Attachment in Children:

- Children with an anxious attachment style tend to experience:
- Anxiety
- Fear of strangers.
- Extreme distress when separated from parents.
- Crying that caregivers cannot easily comfort.
- Clinging to parents and caregivers.
- Not exploring as much as other children.
- Difficulty controlling negative emotions.
- Poor relationships with other children.
- Signs of Anxious Attachment in Adults:
- Adults with an anxious attachment style tend to have.
- Behaviors that smother or drive their partner away.
- Constant need for contact and support from others.
- Fear of being underappreciated.
- Feeling unsure if a partner can be counted on.

- Hypersensitivity to rejection and abandonment.
- Need to increase feelings of security.
- Negative self-view or self-worth.
- A positive view of one's partner.
- Vigilance to signs that a partner is pulling away.
- Worry over losing a partner.
- Yearning to feel closer and more secure with other.

Feelings of worry and anxiety often intensify when we find ourselves facing certain situations alone. It is natural to feel concerned about being alone in life, which can sometimes lead us to make unhealthy choices, seek validation from others, and develop fears about potential loss or abandonment. These insecurities may stem from experiences in childhood and persist into adulthood, shaping our feelings of ourselves and our relationships.

Becoming Aware of the Concept of Anxious Attachment

Until my granddaughter shared her experiences with me, I was unaware of the concept of anxious attachment. She confided that when she wasn't in the presence of family members, she would experience intense nervousness, a feeling that escalated during the COVID-19 pandemic. The thought of being left alone caused her significant distress, even leading to panic attacks. As I listened to her, I couldn't help but reflect on the biblical teachings that encourage us not to worry or be anxious about anything. Instead, we are recommended to bring our concerns to God through prayer and petition while keeping an attitude of gratitude.

These words from the Bible hold a profound wisdom that can guide us in times of anxiety and uncertainty. They remind us that we don't have to bear the weight of our worries alone. Through prayer, we can find solace and seek divine intervention. It is through this connection with God that we can express our concerns, hopes, and fears, trusting that He is attentive and lovingly present.

As I contemplate my granddaughter's struggles with anxious attachment, I am reminded of the power of faith and the importance of seeking support and understanding. Through empathy and compassion, we can supply a nurturing environment that fosters a sense of security and reassurance. Additionally, encouraging her to cultivate a relationship with God, where she can find comfort and peace, may help alleviate her anxious thoughts and bring about a sense of serenity.

Together, we can navigate these challenges, understanding that anxiety is a common human experience. By drawing strength from our faith and embracing the teachings of the Bible, we can find the courage to face our worries, entrusting them to a higher power and finding hope in the journey ahead.

When we are on our own, the weight of responsibility and decision-making can feel overwhelming. We may question our ability to handle life's challenges without someone by our side. This fear of being alone can push us into seeking companionship, sometimes even in relationships that may not be healthy or fulfilling. We may believe that being with someone, even if the relationship is not ideal, is better than being alone.

Validation from others becomes crucial when we lack confidence in ourselves. We seek reassurance and approval from external sources to fill the void of self-doubt and insecurity. We may rely on others' opinions and feedback to figure out our worth, leading to a cycle of seeking constant validation and approval.

The worry about something happening to a loved one or being left alone reflects a deep-seated fear of loss and abandonment. These concerns can be rooted in past experiences where we felt abandoned or unsupported. Childhood experiences play a significant role in shaping our attachment patterns and can contribute to feelings of insecurity and fear in adulthood.

To address these concerns, it is essential to recognize and understand the origins of these insecurities. Therapy or counseling can supply a safe space to explore and work through these underlying issues, helping to build self-esteem, develop healthier relationship patterns, and address any unresolved childhood traumas. It is crucial to develop a sense of self-worth that is not dependent on external validation and to cultivate self-compassion and self-reliance.

Remember, it is possible to overcome these insecurities and fears. Building a supportive network of friends and loved ones who value and appreciate us for who we are can help alleviate feelings of loneliness. By focusing on personal growth, self-care, and nurturing healthy relationships, we can gradually develop a sense of security, resilience, and confidence in navigating life's challenges independently.

Journal

Let Us Practice:

What is an idea or project that you have or may have started working on and have not completed?

_____

_____

_____

_____

_____

_____

What has caused you to get stuck with this idea? Is there another way to approach the problem?

_____

_____

_____

_____

_____

_____

Can I (Meaning Myself) Give Any Suggestions in Helping with this Idea?

_____

_____

_____

_____

_____

Chapter 41

Mindful Meditation

What is Mindful Meditation?

Mindful meditation is when you sit down and reflect on Relax and Renew your mind. You find a quiet space in your home, park, or somewhere where you can get away from the hustle and bustle of the day and spend time with yourself.

How do I Start Mindful meditation?

You can start your mindful meditation on your lunch break or wherever you can find time to spend time with you for at least 10-20 minutes or however long you have.

You can go onto YouTube or any music platform and find relaxing affirmations to listen to.

A Simple Meditation Practice

1. Sit comfortably...

2. Notice what your legs are doing...

3. Straighten your upper body—but do not stiffen...

4. Notice what your arms are doing...

5. Soften your gaze...

6. Feel your breath...

7. Notice when your mind wanders from your breath...

8. Be kind about your wandering mind...

How did you Feel After Your Meditation?

_____

_____

_____

_____

_____

_____

_____

_____

_____

_____

_____

_____

_____

_____

_____

_____

_____

_____

_____

_____

_____

_____

_____

_____

_____

Chapter 42

You Need to Love You

Loving yourself after experiencing trauma is a challenging journey. Trauma can take various forms, such as bullying or assault. However, it is possible to cultivate self-love through learning and practicing self-care. So, how can you embark on this journey of self-love?

Firstly, forgiving the perpetrator and you is a crucial step. Remember, what happened to you was not your fault. Release any guilt or shame that you may carry, recognizing that you did not choose or deserve the trauma that occurred.

Self-healing plays a vital role in your recovery. Each morning, stand before the mirror and affirm that today is a good day. Remind yourself that you are beautiful and worthy of love. As you learn to love and embrace yourself, others will be naturally drawn to your authentic radiance.

Let go of any resentment towards those who have tried to harm you. Acknowledge that their actions cannot destroy your spirit because you are loved. Embrace your inherent worthiness and recognize that your beauty goes beyond external appearances. Even if others do not see it, it does not diminish your value.

Practice self-affirmation and speak positive words about yourself. You have a voice that deserves to be heard, and you should never allow anyone to undermine or project their issues onto you. Take control of your own life, set up healthy boundaries, and prioritize self-care. Remember, it is okay to say "no" when necessary. When you embrace your right to say "no" and stand up for yourself, you will feel empowered and aligned with what is right for you.

Throughout this journey, be patient with yourself. Healing takes time, and there may be setbacks along the way. Seek support from trusted friends, family, or professionals who can guide you through the process. Remember, you deserve love, respect, and happiness. As you continue to practice self-love, you will discover your own inner strength and resilience.

"You Need to Learn to Love You, Too"

In a world where Love is sought after,
Why do we rely on others to say, "I love you?"

Anger and illness breed bitterness,
Born from the trauma we have endured.

But Love, Oh Love, it shines through,
Radiating from the inside out.

In your presence, others see something special,
A youthfulness that belies your years.

Your actions speak volumes, different from the bitter,
For you know your true self, unwavering.

No need to fight for Love's embrace,
For it is others who fight to be loved by you.

Love knows no conditions,
It flows freely, and you, in turn, give Love without reserve.

Yet sometimes Love stings, like a birthing pain,
But soon the anguish subsides, leaving only joy.

As you gaze upon your child's face,
Love fills your heart, erasing all the pain.

If only we could live our lives this way,
Speaking what needs to be said, focusing on the good.

Remember the goodness before the hurt,
Let the pain fade into the background.

For the vast majority of good outweighs the hurt,
Yet we often fixate on that small fraction of pain.

To love others, you must first Love yourself,
And forgiveness becomes the key.

Without Love, there is no true existence,
But with Love, we find everlasting bliss.

©Copyright by Valerie Kelso, I Love You

Chapter 43

Positive Affirmations

- My mind is at peace
- It is my right to feel comfortable
- It is all right to allow for change in my life
- I have the right to be me
- I love myself
- I can go beyond my fears and limitations
- I have the right to express my anger and

work through it

- I have the right to choose my friend.

Are These Your Beliefs?

- My friends do not support me.
- I have no one to talk or listen to me.
- I am the wrong size and shape.
- I am not good enough.
- I am afraid of rejection.
- I cannot be myself.
- How can someone love me.
- Nobody ever asks me what I think.
- My parents hate me.
- I am not as good has my siblings.
- My clothes are not good enough.
- My teacher hates me.

Chapter 44

Negative Beliefs Can Destroy Your Confidence

Negative beliefs have the power to dismantle your confidence, but it's crucial to counteract them with positive thinking. Refuse to let anyone undermine your sense of self-worth.

Your mindset plays a pivotal role in shaping your confidence. When negative beliefs take root, they can erode your self-assurance and hinder your personal growth. The key is to actively replace those negative thoughts with positive affirmations and constructive perspectives.

In the face of external criticism or discouragement, it's essential to fortify your mental resilience. Recognize that you have the agency to shape your own narrative. Choose to focus on your strengths, accomplishments, and the potential for growth rather than succumbing to detrimental beliefs.

Surround yourself with a supportive environment that encourages positivity. Seek out individuals who uplift and inspire you, and distance yourself from those who perpetuate negativity. Building a strong support system contributes significantly to fostering a positive mindset.

Remember that confidence is an inside job. It starts with how you perceive yourself. Embrace your uniqueness, celebrate your achievements, and be kind to yourself in moments of challenge. By cultivating self-compassion, you create a foundation for enduring confidence

Challenge negative beliefs by questioning their validity. Are they based on facts, or are they distorted perceptions? Engage in a constructive inner dialogue that promotes self-awareness and challenges unfounded negativity. This process allows you to reclaim control over your thoughts and beliefs.

Ultimately, your confidence is a reflection of your self-perception. Choose to think positively, nurture your self-worth, and stand firm against external influences that seek to undermine your confidence. The path to true confidence involves embracing a positive mindset, cultivating resilience, and fostering an environment that supports your personal growth.

Self-Love

At times, self-reflection becomes essential
to unravel the reasons behind how we feel.

Questions serve as a compass,
guiding our way to understand the root causes we must convey.

Why do these emotions weigh heavily on my chest?
What hidden issues within me need to be addressed?

Am I internalizing problems that are not truly there?
How can I overcome obstacles and break free from despair?

Find the challenges you currently face,
Acknowledge the struggles within your own space.

Are they born from external sources or self-made?
Unraveling the truth, do not be afraid.

It is self-doubt, holding you back,
or fear of failure, veering off the track.
Unresolved conflicts or past wounds still raw,
Understanding the issues is the first step you draw.

Take a moment to pause, listen to your heart,
in quiet reflection, let self-awareness impart.

Find the burdens that hinder your way
and seek the clarity that will pave a new day.

Remember, you have the strength to persevere,
to face the challenges and overcome fear.

Take that step back, ask yourself with care,
Discover the answers that will lead you there.

Chapter 45

Do Not Let Your Feelings Consume You

Feeling alone can be all-consuming, but remember, you hold the power within. Break free from the cycle, step out of your own way, for only you can shape your destiny each day.

Rise and shine with purpose; make your day shine; your actions and demeanor will guide the way. Choose to be grumpy, and the day will follow suit, but with a positive attitude, you will find your day's route.

Embrace the morning with optimism and cheer. Watch as time flies by, with energy clear. Your aura will radiate, touching those around you; try it for two weeks, and let your journal astound.

Record each day's journey, note how it goes, and the impact of positivity; only time will show.

As you seize control, influencing feeling, See the transformation, feel the connection.

So let go of the doubts, release the negative sway, take charge of your life, create a brighter display. With each morning's sunrise, a chance to renew, you hold the key to shaping a day that is true.

Journal

Thank You

Thank you for the chance to share information and help you heal from your earlier abuse or traumatic event. We hope you have been given the tools necessary to build a solid foundation of successful living and will continue to reach out if you need more help. Our supporters because Silence Hides Violence. Abuse hurts Everyone.

Disclaimer: This book serves to be a general guide for our recovery program. The actual program schedule and content can and will be adjusted to meet your needs.

DIRECTORY

Department of Family & Protective Services - Child Abuse

(800) 252-5400

Online: Texas Abuse Hotline

Day One Services - Economic Abuse Crisis Hotline

(866) 223-1111

Email: Safety@dayoneservices.org

Emotional Abuse and Psychological Abuse - Crisis Text Line

Text Home to 741741 to speak to a crisis counselor

Foster Care Abuse - Texas Dept. of Family and Protective Services

(800) 252-5400

TX. Abuse Hotline - Call 911 for emergencies

National Domestic Violence Hotline

Support, resources, and advice for your safety

1-800-799-SAFE (7233)

National Institute on Drug Abuse

Adolescent Drug and Alcohol Abuse

SAMHSA's National Hotline

(800) 662-Help (4357)

**NORTH TEXAS ADDICTION COUNSELING
& EDUCATION, INC.** - Health and Medical
124 W. Pioneer Pkwy STE. 120
Arlington, TX 76010
(817) 795-8278
www.ntace.org

NORTHSIDE COMMUNITY HEALTH CENTER - Health and
Medical
2106 N. Main St.
Fort Worth, TX 76164
(817) 625-4254
www.aghc.org

NORTH RICHLAND HILLS BAPTIST CHURCH - Education: ESL
and U.S. Citizenship Classes, Food
6955 BOULEVARD 26
North Richland Hills, TX 76180
(817) 284-9206
www.nrhbc.org

N.IC.A - NORTHSIDE INTER-CHURCH AGENCY - Emergency/Food

Clothing, Hygiene Issues

1600 Circle Park Blvd.

Fort Worth, TX 76164

(817) 626-1102

Website: www.nicaagency.org

Email: info@niccagency.org

Office of Trafficking in Persons

National Human Trafficking Hotline

(888) 373-7888

Email: help@humantraffickinghotline.org

Text: help to 233733 (BEFREE)

ONE SAFE PLACE - Domestic Violence

1100 Hemphill

Fort Worth, Texas 76104

(817) 916-4323

PEACE LUTHERAN CHURCH - Food, Health and Medical:

Prescriptions, Housing and Rental Assistance

941 Bedford- Euless Rd.

Hurst, TX 76053

(817) 284-1677

PILGRIM VALLEY MISSIONARY BAPTIST CHURCH -
Counseling: Substance Abuse, Food
4800 S. Riverside Dr.
Fort Worth, TX 76119
(817) 535-8631

PREGNANCY LIFELINE - Pregnancy
4747 S. Hulen STE. 103
Fort Worth, TX 76132
(817) 292-6449
Website: www.pregnancylifeline.net
Email: life103@swbell.net

PREGNANCY HELP CENTER - Pregnancy
7700-A Camp Bowie W.
Fort Worth, TX 76116
(817) 560-2226
(817) 846-4657 (24hr Hotline)
Website: www.phcfw.org
Email: phcfwx@att.net

SAFE HAVEN OF TARRANT COUNTY - Advocacy, Counseling,
Emergency/Crisis Issues, Legal Assistance
8701 Bedford-Euless Rd. Suite 600
Hurst, TX 76053
(817) 535-6462

SANTA FE YOUTH SERVICES - Youth Services

All Services Are Free - counseling for abuse, addiction, tragedy, etc.

7524 Mosier View Court #200

Fort Worth, TX 76118

(817) 492-HOPE /4673 Main

(817) 492-8974 Fax

www.santafeyouth.org

SHAKEN BABY ALLIANCE - Advocacy: Child Abuse Prevention

8551 Boat Club Rd STE. 117

Fort Worth, TX 76135

(817) 882-8686 Main

(817) 882-8687 Fax

Website: www.shakenbaby.org

ST. JOHN'S OUTREACH

JOHN THE APOSTLE CATHOLIC CHURCH

(Food, Health and Medical: Prescriptions, Pregnancy: Baby Items)

7337 Glenview Dr.

North Richland Hills, TX 76180

(817) 284-5912

www.sjtanrh.com

SUICIDE & CRISIS CENTER OF NORTH TEXAS -

Emergency/Crisis Issues

(800) 273-8255 /TALK Toll-Free National Suicide Prevention Hotline

(214) 828-1000 24 Hour Crisis Hotline www.sccenter.org

TARRANT COUNTY DOMESTIC RELATIONS OFFICE - Child
Support Assistance, Legal Assistance
200 E. Weatherford, Second floor
Fort Worth, TX 76102
(817) 884-1111

TARRANT COUNTY PUBLIC HEALTH DEPARTMENT - Health
and Medical
1101 S. Main Street Fort Worth, TX 76104
(817) 321-4700 Main
(817) 321-5400 Appointment Line/WIC
(817) 248-6299 COVID-19 Hotline
(817) 321-4808 HIV/AIDS, Preventive Medicine
(817) 321-5311 Immunization Information Line
(817) 321-4803 STD Clinic
(817) 321-4900 TB Clinic
(817) 321-4707 Travel Health
access.tarrantcounty.com/en/public-
health.html/57ww.tarrantcounty.com/eDRO

TARRANT COUNTY
CCMS - Recovery Childcare
305 NE Loop 820 #1
Hurst, TX 76053
817-831-0374

TEXANS CAN! ACADEMY - Education

6620 Westcreek Dr.

Fort Worth, TX 76133

817-531-3223

www.texanscan.org

www.fortworthcan.org

THE PARENTING CENTER - Counseling, Marriage and Relationships,

Parenting, Pregnancy

2928 W. Fifth St.

Fort Worth, TX 76107

(817) 332-6348 Main

(817) 332-6399 Parenting Advice Line

(800) 369-4230 Toll Free

www.theparentingcenter.org

THE WARM PLACE -WHAT ABOUT REMEMBERING ME -

Counseling: Grief Support Center for Children

809 Lipscomb St.

Fort Worth, TX 76104

(817) 870-2272 Main

Website: www.thewarmplace.org

Email: info@thewarmplace.org

THE WOMEN'S CENTER OF TARRANT COUNTY - Advocacy, Counseling, Emergency, Employment and Training: for Men and Women, Legal Assistance

1723 Hemphill

Fort Worth, TX 76110

(817) 927-4006 Administration

(817) 927-4000 Helpline

(817) 927-4050 Employment Solutions

(817) 927-2737 Rape Crisis & Victim Service Hotline

Website: www.womenscentertc.org

Email: info@womencenterc.org

THERAPEUTIC FAMILY LIFE - Adoption/Foster Care, Youth Services

Corporate Center Building II

1112 E. Copeland Suite 420

Arlington, TX 76011

(817) 265-2328 Main

TRAUMA SUPPORT SERVICES OF NORTH TEXAS - Advocacy, Counseling, Emergency/Crisis Issues

210 S. Cedar Ridge Dr. - Suite C-100

Duncanville, TX. 75116

(817) 378-7158 Main/(972) 709-4904 Alternate

Website: www.tssnt.org

Email: tssnt@att.net

TRINITY HABITAT FOR HUMANITY - Housing

93330N Normandale

Fort Worth, TX 76116

(817) 926-9219 Main

Website: www.trinityhabitat.org

Email: info@trinityhabitat.org

UNION GOSPEL MISSION - Food

1321 East Lancaster

 Fort Worth, TX 76102

(817) 339-2553 Main

(817) 332-1437 Donations (financial)

(817) 284-3255 Donations (goods for pick up)

(817) 332-3019 M.J. Neely Men's Building

(817) 332-7531 Women's Center

www.ugm-tc.org

UNITED COMMUNITY CENTERS, INC. - After-School Programs,

Youth Services

1200 E. Maddox

 Fort Worth, TX 76104

(817) 927-5556 Main

www.unitedcommunitycenters.org

UNITED WAY OF TARRANT COUNTY - Advocacy, Information and Referral

1500 N. Main - Suite 200

Fort Worth, TX 76164

(817) 258-8000

www.unitedwaytarrant.org

UNT HEALTH SCIENCE CENTER - Health and Medical

855 Montgomery St.

Fort Worth, TX 76107

(817) 735-3627

www.hsc.unt.edu

VICTORY TEMPLE MINISTRIES - Emergency/Crisis Issues

2526 Columbus

Fort Worth, TX 76164

(817) 626-1819 Main

Website: www.victorytempleministries.com

Email: info@victorytempleministries.com

VOLUNTEERS OF AMERICA - Emergency/Crisis Issues, Youth
Services
300 E. Midway Dr.
Euless, TX 76039
(817) 529-7300
www.voatx.org
Website: www.thewarmplace.org
Email: info@thewarmplace.org

WATER FROM THE ROCK - Education: Job Workshops, GED,
Computer Training, Food and Clothing
1015 Gibbons Road
Arlington, TX 76011
(817) 860-9702
Email: waterfromtherock2u@sbcglobal.net

WEE-CARE PANTRY - Food and Clothing: Clothing for Infants and
Small Children
3141 Carson St.
Haltom City, TX 76117
(817) 831-0586

WESLEY MISSION CENTER - Emergency/Crisis Issues, Food
777 N. Walnut Creek Drive
Mansfield, TX 76063
(817) 473-6650
www.wesleymissioncenter.org

WEST AID - JPS Viola Pitts Clinic - Health and Medical Services
7940 Camp Bowie West
 Fort Worth, TX 76116
(817) 737-9338
www.westaid.org
Email: westaid@sbcglobal.net

WEST FREEWAY CHURCH OF CHRIST - Food and Clothing
8000 Western Hills Boulevard
Fort Worth, TX 76108
(817) 246-8000
www.wfcoc.org

WHEN WE LOVE - Food, Clothing, Rental Assistance, Information &
Referrals
1100 E. Lancaster Ave.
Fort Worth, TX 76102
(817) 503-5185
www.whenwelove.org
info@whenwelove.org

WHITE SETTLEMENT INDEPENDENT SCHOOL DISTRICT -
Education
401 South Cherry Lane
White Settlement, TX 76108-2521
(817) 367-1300
www.wsisd.com

WIC of TARRANT COUNTY
6601 Watauga Road
Watauga, TX 76148
817-321-5400

WISH WITH WINGS, INC. - Youth Services
917 West Sanford Street
Arlington, TX 76012
(817) 469-9474
Website: www.awishwithwings.org
Email: wish@awishwithwings.org

WOMEN'S CHOICE RESOURCE CENTER - Emergency/Crisis
Issues, Information and Referral, Pregnancy
324 Rand St.
Fort Worth, TX 76103
(817) 534-9947
www.choicepregnancy.com

WORKFORCE SOLUTIONS FOR TARRANT COUNTY - Childcare, Employment and Training: Job Search, Veterans and Military Families, Youth Services

Locations throughout Tarrant County

(817) 413-4400/(817) 413-4000 (alternate)

(817) 420-1600 (Unemployment Insurance)

Website: www.workforcesolutions.net

Email: info@workforcesolutions.net

YMCA OF ARLINGTON - After-School Programs, Youth Services

1148 W. Pioneer Pkwy STE. H

Arlington, TX 76013

(817) 299-9629 Main

Website: www.ymca-arlington.org

YMCA OF METROPOLITAN FORT WORTH - After-School Programs, Youth Services

512 Lamar Street,

Suite 400

Fort Worth, TX 76102

(817) 332-3281 Main

Website: www.ymcafw.org

YWCA FORT WORTH & TARRANT COUNTY - After-School
Programs, Childcare, Youth Services
512 West 4th Street
Fort Worth, TX 76102
(817) 332-6191 Main
Website: www.ywcafortworth.org
Email: ywca@ywcafortworth.org

ABOUT THE AUTHOR

I'm Valerie Kelso, born in England, and I'm a mother to my daughter Rachael, as well as a proud grandmother to two beautiful granddaughters, Taisha and Teoni. The inspiration behind writing this book stems from the realization that, too often, individuals endure abuse because they believe there's no escape. In these pages, I aim to delve into the complexities of relationships, abuse, and divorce, drawing from my own experiences.

Despite growing up in a household where my parents did not abuse each other, I found myself in an abusive relationship. Through sharing my personal journey, I hope to shed light on the intricacies of abuse, referencing insights from the Bible and emphasizing the importance of gaining control over one's life. The narrative explores how, despite seemingly protective backgrounds, we can still find ourselves in harmful situations. My intention is to empower readers to take charge of their lives and refuse to tolerate any form of abuse, emphasizing the significance of self-control and the Biblical perspective on the matter.

www.ingramcontent.com/pod-product-compliance
Lightning Source LLC
Chambersburg PA
CBHW051150120626
46547CB00012B/1026